THE RECOVERING HEART

THE RECOVERING HEART

Emotional Sobriety for Women

Beverly Conyers

Hazelden
Publishing

Hazelden Publishing
Center City, Minnesota 55012
hazelden.org/bookstore

Library of Congress Cataloging-in-Publication Data
Conyers, Beverly.
        The recovering heart : emotional sobriety for women / Beverly Conyers.
            pages cm
        Summary: "You are finally sober and drug-free. Your old, destructive lifestyle is
fading into the past and now you are a woman in recovery. What an amazing gift
you've given yourself. So why aren't you happier? As sobriety takes hold and your
head starts to clear, a wide range of emotions can begin to emerge-feelings that until
now you've 'medicated' with chemicals. Yet to stay sober, and to grow and flourish
as a person, you must engage in healing and take responsibility for these emotions
that have been neglected since you first starting using. Beverly Conyers, a prominent
voice in recovery, uses personal stories and informed insight to guide you in achieving
emotional sobriety by addressing behaviors and feelings unique to the female
experience. Learn how to develop the inner resiliency to face and process difficult,
buried emotions-such as shame, grief, fear, and anger-while freeing the positive feelings
of self-worth, independence, and integrity. Discover how to heal your 'damaged self'
by improving your communication skills, expanding your capacity for intimacy and
trust, and reawakening a spiritual life. It is through your own personal journey of
healing your wounded heart that you can free yourself to a life of self-acceptance,
and lay the foundation for a rewarding and relapse-free second stage of recovery."
—Provided by publisher.
        Summary: "Offering guidance to women in recovery from alcoholism or other
addictions, Beverly Conyers gives readers wisdom for the journey. She depicts several
recovering women and their hard-won lessons, showing how they overcame trauma
to regain their self-respect and lead productive, joyful lives."—Provided by publisher.
            ISBN 978-1-61649-437-7 (pbk.) — ISBN 978-1-61649-497-1 (ebook)
        1. Self-esteem in women. 2. Self-perception in women. 3. Recovering addicts.
I. Title.
        BF697.5.S46C666 2013
        616.86'03082—dc23

                                        2012049787

Cover design by Percolator
Interior design and typesetting by Madeline Berglund

*And the day came when the risk
to remain tight in a bud was more painful
than the risk it took to blossom.*

ANAÏS NIN

*For M.V. and women everywhere who face
the darkness and find their inner light*

Contents

Acknowledgments

I am amazed and humbled by the generosity, honesty, and courage of the women who shared their stories for this book. They lived through long periods of pain, shame, and despair. Many of them faced rejection, abuse, and devastating losses. Worst of all, most of them came to doubt the value of their own existence.

Yet, each of these women found within herself some kernel of inner strength—a stubborn refusal to be destroyed by what had hurt her. By daring to believe in the possibility of a better life, they worked through their fears, overcame setbacks, and slowly moved toward a place of healing and self-affirmation.

In telling their stories, these incredible women revealed their hard-earned wisdom and opened my eyes to the boundless potential of the human spirit. I learned much more from them than I could have anticipated at the beginning of this journey. For showing me what healing really means, I thank them from the bottom of my heart.

To protect their privacy, I have changed some identifying details about the women in this book. Most of the names that appear were chosen by the women themselves.

INTRODUCTION

What scares me is that I'm going to ultimately find out at the end of my life that I'm really not lovable, that I'm not worthy of being loved. That there's something fundamentally wrong with me.

—DEMI MOORE,
actress, Harper's Bazaar *interview, 2012*

Loneliness. Fear. Self-doubt. Self-criticism. These feelings lie at the heart of the shadowy inner world of many women today—even women who seem to have it all. Regardless of how successful we may appear to others or how much we've accomplished in our lives, we're often our most determined detractor, our most unforgiving critic.

We might catch a glimpse of ourselves in a mirror and think, "I look old and tired. I look fat." Or we lose a job through no fault of our own and tell ourselves, "I'm a failure. I can't do anything right." Perhaps our marriage ends or we yell at our children and we conclude, "I'm a terrible person. I don't deserve to be loved."

For women in recovery from addictions to alcohol, drugs, food, and compulsive behaviors, this painful self-criticism goes even deeper. Our life experiences have led us to question our own value, to deny our fundamental worth as a human being. Many of us were subjected to some sort of trauma at a critical point in our development, often at the hands of someone we trusted. Trauma damages our core sense of self and fills us with shame.

Our addictions inflicted new traumas: fractured relationships, public and private humiliations, and lost opportunities. On top of all that, we bear the stigma of being a woman with addictions.

All addictions carry some degree of stigma, whether the addict is male or female. But a greater stigma is attached to women. According to the National Institute on Alcohol Abuse and Alcoholism, there are about 18 million alcoholics or problem drinkers in the United States.[1] By some estimates, about a third of them are women. Yet Al-Anon membership is overwhelmingly female. (Al-Anon is a mutual support group for friends and families of problem drinkers.) Shame surely plays a role in men's reluctance to publicly acknowledge and seek help for the problem of an alcoholic partner.

We can also see the stigma of female addiction in the public's response to celebrities with substance abuse problems. Consider the well-publicized struggles of actors Charlie Sheen and Lindsay Lohan. Many people seemed to regard Sheen's antics as nothing worse than the hijinks of a notorious "bad boy." Lohan, on the other hand, garnered widespread ridicule for her many failed attempts to get clean.

As one alcoholism counselor put it, "A man who falls down drunk is still a man, but a woman who falls down drunk is a tramp." The double standard was also observed by the late Carolyn Knapp, who wrote in her memoir *Drinking: A Love Story,* "A messy drunk's an ugly thing, especially when it's a woman."[2]

For women with addictions, the stigma becomes part of our self-identity, further damaging our already shaky emotional inner world. Our fear and our pain and our shame saturate the very core of our being, shaping our decisions, coloring our relationships, and defining who we think we are—sometimes even after years of living clean and sober. But that's hardly surprising, especially when we think about women in recovery within the broader context of womanhood today. "Traditional" and "modern" interpretations of femininity have been at odds for generations. In the mid-1800s, women's rights activist Susan B. Anthony wrote, "Modern invention has banished the spinning wheel, and the same law of progress makes the woman of today a different woman from her grandmother." A century later,

First Lady Bess Truman observed, "A woman's place in public is to sit beside her husband, be silent, and be sure her hat is on straight."

Since then, the emergence of feminism and the entry of millions of women into the workforce have given us a sense of empowerment that our grandmothers probably never had. Still, like generations of women before us, we are bombarded with confusing and contradictory messages about our value to society. It can sometimes feel as though womanhood itself is under attack.

On one hand, we are expected to be nurturing, pleasant, and wholesome (hence the stigma for female addicts). On the other hand, pornography permeates our culture and degrades the value of women. We are expected to be chaste and at the same time sexually proficient. We are told it's our minds, not our bodies, that matter, yet we are judged by our physical attractiveness. We are taught that we are men's equal, yet violence against women remains an ugly fact of life for millions of us. We are the breadwinner or partial breadwinner in our families, but women still are not equally compensated for doing the same work as men. Arguably, our central role in mainstream society remains that of homemaker and mother.

In this minefield of conflicting messages, is it any wonder why so many women struggle to develop a healthy sense of their own worth? For women in recovery, who have spent years numbing and running away from difficult emotions, the task is even harder. We have used alcohol, drugs, food, shopping, sex, codependence, and other substances and behaviors to avoid and distract ourselves from the wounds at our core. We have little or no practice with confronting painful feelings in ways that contribute to our personal growth.

Our early days of recovery provided yet another avenue of escape from upsetting emotions. We were physically and mentally stressed, and we focused all our energy on staying clean and sober, one day at a time. And rightly so. Abstinence is the goal of early recovery. Little else can be achieved without it.

But as time passes and we become more secure in our recovery, long-buried feelings inevitably emerge. Wounds from the past are still deep inside us, unexamined, untended, and unhealed. The harm we have done to ourselves and to others is waiting to be acknowledged, understood, and mended.

At this point some of us are tempted to relapse, to retreat to the familiar numbing comfort of substances or compulsive behaviors. This is understandable. Nothing has prepared us for the difficulty of confronting painful memories head-on. We never learned how to face the source of our anger and grief and remorse or to fully feel our emotions. We are frightened by what has hurt us in the past and uncertain of our ability to cope with it.

Yet personal growth requires us to stop running and start engaging in the process of facing our emotions—not so we can wallow in pain or relive the trauma, but so we can move beyond it and become our healthy, authentic self.

Most of our ideas about who we are—whether we call ourselves good or bad, strong or weak, worthy or unworthy—come from our *feelings* about ourselves. These feelings, which begin in infancy and develop throughout our lives, determine our understanding of who we are. And who we think we are—*how we see ourselves*—influences every choice we make, from our choice of education and career to our decisions about relationships and self-care.

That's why emotional healing is so powerful. Personal growth cannot happen without it. Until we untangle the web of hurtful and damaging emotions that prevent us from seeing ourselves clearly, we will continue to suffer from our secret belief that something is wrong with us. And that belief will prevent us from achieving our full potential or recognizing our true value as a unique, worthwhile person.

The Twelve Steps are not only a path to freedom from our addictions, they also offer guideposts to emotional healing, gently leading us to higher levels of understanding and self-awareness. Professional therapists also offer support and guidance. Good therapists let us explore our emotions at our own pace and in our own way, understanding that emotional healing cannot be rushed. It unfolds differently for every woman.

This book is offered as a companion for your journey, not to provide answers—those you will discover for yourself—but to suggest avenues of exploration and to share the experiences of others on the same path. At the end of each chapter you'll find several journal questions. These are meant to stimulate ideas to write about or discuss with a trusted mentor or therapist. Use them only to the extent that you find them helpful.

Ultimately, the journey of emotional healing is deeply personal—and it is the work of a lifetime. Our search for our own truths and our own meaning, once begun, never really ends, because the accumulation of experience and knowledge cannot help but affect our understanding of ourselves and others. The way we think about something at the age of thirty is likely to be different by the time we reach sixty.

Nevertheless, as we acknowledge, examine, and come to terms with the feelings we have tried so hard to run away from, we can begin to free ourselves of old, negative misperceptions about ourselves. We start to see ourselves more clearly and to recognize our own strengths, values, and virtues.

As our wounded heart begins to heal, we take our first small, courageous, wonderfully liberating steps towards self-acceptance, personal fulfillment, and spiritual wholeness.

1

THE HEART OF THE MATTER

*I almost think I can remember feeling
a little different. But if I'm not the same,
the next question is "Who in the world am I?"
Ah, that's the great puzzle!*

—ALICE,
in Lewis Carroll's Alice in Wonderland

O ne bright Saturday morning, my friend Meg and I were taking a walk around our neighborhood. It was one of those perfect spring days when puffs of white clouds sail through the sky and a warm breeze stirs the green-gold trees.

I love spring. Something about the hopefulness of it makes me happy. But that day, I could tell Meg was troubled. Normally a lively and talkative person, Meg seemed quiet and sad. "I'm not very good company today," she muttered after a while.

I asked if something was bothering her.

She gave a little sigh. "I was looking through some old photos last night. I don't know why. Masochism, maybe. I found one of me and my mom I'd forgotten about. I'm about six and we're on the beach and I'm glaring at the camera like I'm pissed off at the world." She shrugged. "I don't know. It reminds me what a miserable brat I was."

"Oh, Meg! You had your reasons."

"Yeah. She was a terror, that's for sure. But at least she didn't end up losing her kids." She gave a pebble an angry kick. "I mean, what kind of piece-of-crap mother does that?"

I stopped and looked her in the eyes. "A mother who's hooked on pills and alcohol," I said firmly. "A mother who's lost her way. But look how far you've come."

She kicked another pebble and fell silent again as we resumed walking.

Meg's life looks good on the outside, but she's struggled emotionally for years. Her mom had been harsh and verbally abusive, her dad abandoned the family when she was eight, and she had her first child at seventeen after a drunken sexual encounter she barely remembered. Still, Meg earned a college degree and built a solid career in hospital administration. By the time she was thirty-five, she was married to a nice guy and had two more kids and a lovely house. She went on great vacations and wore pretty clothes and drove a new car.

She was living the American dream—except for an addiction to alcohol and benzodiazepines (tranquilizers) that she managed to keep hidden for years.

I didn't know her then, but Meg says that when she crashed, it was ugly. Her temper became explosive and her moods swung between rage and despair. She lost her job. Her husband divorced her and won custody of the kids. David, the youngest, said he was scared of her.

At the age of forty, she was living in a women's shelter and asking herself how it had come to this. But Meg's a fighter, and slowly she climbed out of the hole she'd fallen into. By the time we met, she'd been in Twelve Step programs for years. I know her as a warm and compassionate woman who has worked very hard to mend her relationship with her children. Meg has a nice condo and loves her job as a manager in a doctor's office. She also has a side business making jewelry, a talent she discovered only after she got clean and sober.

Still, there are lots of days when Meg doesn't like herself very much.

"We all make mistakes," I reminded her as we walked. "But you learned from yours. You changed. I think that's something to be proud of. "

"I know," she nodded. "I know it up here." She tapped the side of her head. "But inside, I'm still the bad little girl. I'm still the bad mother."

I knew what she meant. I've experienced it myself. I can put on a good game face and present myself as confident and capable when I need to. I can look like I have it all together. But deep inside, a voice sometimes says that something's wrong with me. That if people knew the real me, they'd reject me.

Lots of women I know feel the same way. Between our external and internal worlds is a nagging disconnect, as if our accomplishments and decency are not as real as the flaws inside us. As Meg puts it, "I know in my head that I'm a good person. I know I have a lot of strengths. That's the thinking part of me. But the feeling part of me doesn't believe it. In my heart, I'm still an undeserving, worthless person."

Where do these feelings come from? How do we come to see ourselves as fundamentally unworthy human beings? And what's the difference between who we really are and who we think we are?

To understand the role our experiences play in how we see ourselves, we have to go back to our earliest childhood. That's when we begin to develop a sense of our own identity.

THE EMERGING SELF

We all come into this world needing safety and security. We need to know that we'll be fed when we're hungry, cleaned when we're soiled, and protected and comforted when we feel threatened or are in pain. Long before we can express our needs with words, we instinctively cry, babble, and smile to attract the attention we need.

As newborns, we have little sense of ourselves as individual beings. Instead, we exist as an extension of our primary caregiver— most often, our mother. This initial bond is so powerful that many psychologists believe it sets the stage for our emerging sense of self and for the quality of our future relationships. If we're lucky enough to be in the care of someone who responds with consistency and sensitivity to our needs, we form a secure attachment to that person.

Secure and Insecure Attachment

For healthy emotional growth, children need to develop secure attachments with others: that's the idea of attachment theory. The child's attachment to the primary caregiver is the most important. The mother or mother figure gives stability to the child's world. The child can always turn to that person for protection and comfort.

From this nurturing base of secure attachment, toddlers feel safe enough to explore their world. They start to gain independence and satisfy their curiosity, knowing they have a safe haven to return to. In other words, healthy dependence promotes healthy independence and the self-confidence that comes with it.

But that curious toddler still needs her mother. In fact, "separation anxiety" in young children is a sign of healthy attachment. When a mother leaves and an infant or toddler cries, that's a sign of deep attachment to her. Gradually, children learn to trust that their mother will return and comfort them. They come to expect that things will work out. They relax, their self-confidence grows, and a sense of optimism takes root.

But what if the mother doesn't provide the comfort and security her child needs? What if the child's anxiety is not soothed? What if the mother is depressed, addicted, or emotionally distant for other reasons?

In these situations, we may develop what psychologists call an insecure attachment, an uneasy bond with our mother that can lead to social and emotional difficulties later on.

Forming a close emotional bond with another person is a basic human need. Psychologists say that it helps ensure our species' survival. Infants and young children literally cannot live without the care and protection of an older person. Our need for attachment is as absolute as our need for water.

"Even when a mother is emotionally distant, inconsistent, or abusive, her children will usually form an attachment to her," notes Marcela, who battled an addiction to alcohol and prescription drugs before becoming a counselor in a women's recovery house. "It's instinctive. But the attachment is damaged. The mother can't be counted on to provide the care her child needs, so the world seems frightening and unpredictable. This instability can undermine the child's ability to trust and can lead to behavioral problems."

Secure attachment promotes independence, self-confidence, and a positive attitude. But insecure attachment can lead to anxiety, rebelliousness, anger, and low self-esteem. Children—even infants—who are not consistently cherished and nurtured may develop troubling behaviors to protect themselves from further harm.

How does maternal depression affect attachment and children's behavior? A 2003 article, "Mother Blues—Child Blues," published by the NYU Child Study Center, explained:

> The attachment relationship serves as a model for subsequent interpersonal relationships and is believed to be an important predictor of a child's future adjustment. Children of depressed mothers have been found to have difficulty in establishing secure relationships, which may put them at risk for later difficulties. Research has identified other areas in which developmental problems may arise. Young children of depressed mothers have been rated as more drowsy, passive, more temperamentally difficult, less able to tolerate separation, more afraid or more anxious, than children of non-depressed mothers.[3]

Marcela has seen such patterns in the children of mothers she works with. With no safe haven to depend on, she says, "A lot of these kids have to make it up as they go along. They're insecure and their behavior is a response to that. Even though they're too little to understand what they're doing, they're subconsciously trying to get the attention they need or avoid rejection and abuse."

For better or worse, the behaviors and expectations we learn in our earliest attachment—whether secure or insecure—become part of our emotional repertoire. We carry them with us into future experiences and relationships.

But our fate is not sealed in the first few years of life. Far from it. In their book *Understanding Attachment and Attachment Disorders,* researchers Vivien Prior and Danya Glaser suggest that only about 65 percent of young children form a secure attachment with their primary caregiver. The rest of us make do with varying degrees of insecure attachment.[4] Parenting is tricky, as those of us who have been there know. Even with the best intentions, a mother may have emotional issues that hinder her parenting skills. Or maybe her parenting style doesn't suit her child's temperament.

We are not, after all, lumps of clay waiting to be molded into whatever our mother wants to makes of us. When we are born, our genes determine our tendencies toward a whole host of personality traits: we are anxious or calm, assertive or passive, cautious or impulsive. (Research also suggests that our genes can make us more prone to addictions, criminality, and depressive disorders.) So, the consistency and quality of care we receive from our mother is only part of the story. We also filter that care through our own inborn personality. One toddler may flourish with a hands-off parenting style, while another may need constant reassurance. In other words, parenting and genetics both play a role in shaping the quality of our earliest attachment.

Furthermore, life circumstances can change the picture. A troubled mother may blossom into a nurturing mother when she gets help for her own problems. Another mother may find that she is less skilled at parenting older children than toddlers. And traumatic events—such as a death, illness, or divorce—may upset the equilibrium of any securely attached child.

But whatever our inborn personality traits or later life events, psychologists agree that forming a secure early attachment with a nurturing adult gives children an emotionally healthy start in life.

Such a primary attachment plants the seeds for trust, for a sense of belonging, and—most important—for seeing ourselves as worthy of love.

But there is much more to the developing self. As we grow out of infancy, we begin to form a stronger sense of ourselves as people who are separate from our primary caregiver. (A two-year-old's constant "no!" is a sign of this emerging self.) And we begin to see how we fit into the bigger world around us.

A Pretty Little Girl

In one of my earliest memories of myself, I am about three years old, wearing a blue cloth coat with a matching cap that fastened under my chin. The outfit was secondhand, a castoff from a neighbor or relative. The first and perhaps only time I wore it, I remember feeling three things: the fact that the outfit was used, and this somehow diminished its attractiveness; my mother disapproved of my wearing it; and—above all else—it made me look awfully pretty.

I remember riding in a car and gazing out the backseat window, my attention captured now and then by a big truck or some structure in the distance. And then my awareness would return to what I was wearing. I would become conscious of myself in a pretty blue coat and I felt a warm, happy sensation, almost as if I were floating. I felt special.

I felt similarly happy a few years later, when I was six and got a pair of new red shoes with buckles. New shoes were a rarity in my family, and their bright color and pretty straps and cutouts made the shoes seem almost magical.

Around this time, too, I remember getting spanked with a ruler by my teacher for something I didn't do. I also recall going by bus to a charity Christmas party for poor children, where the nuns gave us presents. I received a doll, which somehow disappeared during the party, and a nun dried my tears and gave me an even better present: a wicker doll buggy that would remain in our family for years.

The kind woman sat beside me on the bus all the way home, and I remember feeling protected and safe.

But in my clearest childhood memories, I'm being picked on at school. My family moved around a lot, so I was forever the new kid. And we were poor, so I wore shabby clothes and was often dirty. One day when I was seven, I joined a bunch of kids racing around the schoolyard playing tag—until one of the boys shouted, "Yuck! Don't touch *her*." I retreated and learned to become ashamed of my rough hands and ugly clothes and unattractiveness.

As the taunting continued and days and weeks turned into months and years, I began to think of myself as someone who wasn't likeable because I wasn't pretty and couldn't fit in to any group. There were popular kids—they were clean and nicely dressed and self-confident. And there were ordinary kids, who weren't as well-dressed or self-confident, but who nevertheless seemed just fine and had a stable circle of friends. And then there were the outcasts—me, and sometimes a few others, who hung around the edges of the playground and walked to and from school alone.

I'm still surprised by the extent to which my sense of self was determined by others in those early years. What was really inside me—my intelligence, my talents, my strengths—was yet to emerge. My ability to discern what is true and what is false was still to be born.

Like most children, I saw myself mostly through the eyes of my parents, other authority figures, and my peers. My parents were strict and disapproving, authority figures criticized me, and other children were cruel. Therefore, I concluded that something was fundamentally wrong with me, that for reasons I could not understand I was unworthy of being loved.

Before I learned the meaning of such words as shame, humiliation, anger, and despair, I felt those emotions. I couldn't put my feelings into words, but they were there, shaping the way I saw myself and damaging my perception of who I thought I was. Many women have told me they felt the same.

As young girls and adolescents, we face the universal task of preparing to take our place in the adult world. In this stage of development, our job is to identify our interests and abilities, expand our knowledge, and build the skills we will need to become self-sufficient adults.

Our sense of self directly affects our success in these endeavors. If we're convinced that we are stupid or that nothing ever goes right for us, we're less likely to try new things or to bounce back from failure. If we've acquired defensive behaviors to protect ourselves from the pain of loss or rejection, we're less likely to develop a social network that can lead to new avenues of exploration. And if we've learned to expect anxiety and distress in our emotional life, we're less likely to build the healthy personal relationships that sustain us during life's inevitable disappointments.

For girls—even those from stable families and secure backgrounds, and those who are popular and fit in with their peers—the monumental challenge of moving from childhood to adulthood is further complicated by the very fact of being female.

Psychologists say that by the age of three, most children have established their gender identity—that is, they tend to behave in ways that reflect culturally accepted gender roles. Generally speaking, little boys are drawn to rough-and-tumble play and games with elements of adventure. Little girls, on the other hand, tend to gravitate towards games involving home and childcare. Although many girls expect to have careers beyond that of homemaker, much of their make-believe world centers on home life. For example, video games that simulate dating and family life—like The Sims, which is wildly popular at the time of this writing—are played primarily by girls and young women. From their earliest years, most girls' sense of self is intrinsically linked with the traditional female role of guardian of family and relationships.

Most young girls also learn that they are expected to conduct themselves in a modest and "ladylike" way. Rowdiness may be acceptable in their male counterparts, but many families still convey the message that girls are supposed to be demure, well-mannered, and quiet—in a word, *nice*. In her groundbreaking 1949 book *The Second Sex,* French philosopher and writer Simone de Beauvoir observed:

> All girls, from the most servile to the haughtiest, learn
> in time that to please they must abdicate . . . The young
> girl . . . [must] repress her spontaneity and replace it
> with the studied grace and charm taught her by her
> elders. Any self-assertion will diminish her femininity
> and her attractiveness.[5]

Of course, there are girls who are outspoken, who excel at sports, and who prefer active pursuits more often associated with masculinity. In a 2008 *Psychology Today* article about tomboys, author Sarah Showfety noted, "In a society that still often expects men to be tough and rugged and women to be gentle and pretty, embracing their inner tomboy allows females to stand out and be rewarded for activities, rather than appearance or demeanor." She went on to say that although almost half of women considered themselves tomboys as children, most girls leave tomboy behavior behind during adolescence, when they face peer pressure to conform to society's definition of femininity: Sugar and spice and everything nice—that's what little girls are made of.[6]

But being nice is not enough. Girls must acquire another attribute in order to earn true acceptance and admiration from authority figures and peers. That attribute is attractiveness.

It's How You Look That Counts

From our early childhood, family members and strangers alike tend to comment on our appearance—"Aren't you a pretty little girl!"—rather than on our intelligence or other qualities. One day when my older daughter was around five, we were walking together and we passed a little girl with long red hair. My daughter, who had beautiful, wavy chestnut hair, looked up at me and asked, "Mommy, is her hair prettier than mine?" She already knew the value of her hair and felt threatened by someone whose hair might be considered more attractive.

One day recently, my four-year-old granddaughter asked me why I was wearing a particular skirt. When I told her I liked the skirt, she matter-of-factly explained that it wasn't a pretty color. I redeemed myself the next day by wearing something she approved of. "You look pretty today!" she exclaimed. She herself favors shoes with sparkles and whimsical dresses in purple or pink.

Although there is evidence that traditionally feminine interests—including the desire to look pretty—are to some extent determined by our biological makeup, our society's obsession with female attractiveness has raised the bar on appearance to unhealthy levels. As girls, we measure ourselves against the manufactured images of perfection that surround us—on websites, in magazines, on billboards, on TV and movie screens—and we see ourselves as deeply flawed in comparison. Even the prettiest girls fret about perceived imperfections such as "fat thighs," "flat chests," or "thin lips."

"I always felt inferior to other girls because of my small breasts," one young woman confides. "The boys called me flat-chested. It was embarrassing."

"I inherited my mother's nose and it's too big by conventional standards," says another. "By the time I was in high school, I was convinced I was ugly. Absolutely hideous."

"My skin used to break out and I got called pizza face," recalls another woman. "I was so ashamed of the way I looked, I cried myself to sleep almost every night."

So pervasive is the emphasis on female attractiveness that in 1993 Rush Limbaugh showed his audience an image of thirteen-year-old Chelsea Clinton and joked, "Socks is the White House cat. But did you know there is also a White House dog?" The remark drew both criticism and laughter. But the message was unmistakable: If we do not meet conventional measures of attractiveness, we are a failure. If we're not pretty enough, we are fair game for ridicule.

Of course, women have been valued for their appearance for centuries. More than 3,000 years ago, Egyptian Queen Nefertiti—whose name means "the beautiful one has arrived"—was renowned for her beauty. The mythical Helen of Troy in ancient Greece won admiration as "the face that launched a thousand ships."

But the advent of magazine ads, movies, television, and today's 24-7 media, especially with Internet access on ubiquitous devices, has steadily increased the pressure on girls to achieve physical perfection. Too many of them starve themselves, color their hair, go to tanning salons, and get plastic surgery at ever younger ages, trying to achieve a look that society deems desirable.

Carol, a yoga instructor and recovering alcoholic who battled bulimia for years, recalls, "I was always the perfect kid, the good student, the student leader. My teachers loved me. I volunteered for everything. But inside, I felt like I wasn't good enough. It was always a struggle to stay skinny. I felt like if I let myself go, I'd become this ugly, worthless person. I had to look good to be good."

The struggle for perfection came to dominate Carol's formative years, as it does for many of us. Whether we focus our energies on being a model citizen, an outstanding student, a superior athlete, or a spectacular beauty—and many girls try to do it all—we measure ourselves against impossible standards set by the media and entertainment industries.

Inevitably, we come up short. By the time we reach our late teens, we are all too likely to carry deep feelings of inadequacy at our core—feelings made more intense by our confusing relationship with the opposite sex.

Sexual Awakenings

Most children engage in some sort of sexual play—"you show me yours and I'll show you mine." These games are expressions of curiosity and have nothing to do with sexual arousal. Playing "doctor" is a way to inspect and compare, to explore the mysteries of being different. It's as innocent as a game of tag or blind man's buff.

But as girls, we gradually come to see our bodies as potential objects of male attention. This budding awareness can be unsettling and even frightening. I remember riding on a city bus with my mother when I was ten or eleven. I was wearing a jumper with no shirt underneath it. My mother looked critically at the bib front, which barely covered my chest, and said, "You're getting too big to wear that." I was deeply embarrassed and, for the first time, ashamed of my exposed body.

A friend of mine recalls an uncle commenting on her "large derriere" when she was eight or nine. "I felt insulted, like I was a piece of furniture or some object he could criticize," she says. "But I also felt like there was something wrong with me, and I started worrying about what I ate."

Another friend recalls walking down the street at age nine or ten and some teenage boys in a passing car shouting a vulgarity at her. "They yelled something like, 'Hey, baby! Wanna lick my—' you-know-what. I was disgusted and shocked. I think that was the first time I felt like an object. The first time I thought that being a girl could be kind of dangerous."

For many of us, we become gradually aware of our bodies as objects of male interest. But for others, that awareness is thrust upon us at an early age.

"When I was three, an uncle sat me on his lap and put his finger inside my underwear," Carol confides. "I remember that it felt invasive, a kind of violation. My parents were in the kitchen. He told me not to tell my mommy and daddy. I never did. I knew instinctively that it was something to be ashamed of."

Her experience is not uncommon. The website Advocates for Youth reports that 12 to 40 percent of women have experienced "at least one instance of sexual abuse in childhood or adolescence."[7]

(We will look at the ramifications of this and other forms of abuse in chapter 2.) And many more of us are exposed to looks, comments, and actions that alert us to our vulnerability.

When I was eight or nine, I was playing alone on the monkey bars on the school playground after hours. A rowdy group of boys from my class came along and started grabbing at my skirt. I was afraid of what they would do to me if I got down, so I tried to kick them away while keeping my balance on the steel bars. Eventually they left, but that is the first time I remember being conscious of the potential menace of male strength. I also worried that because they had seen my underwear I might become pregnant—an early hint of the unequal consequences of sexual behavior.

As little girls, we may see ourselves as boys' equals—or even their superiors when it comes to behavior, cleanliness, and intelligence. But the physiological changes of adolescence can bring us face-to-face with our physical limitations. Generally speaking, boys grow to become stronger, faster, and bigger than we are. Even the most dedicated female fitness enthusiasts eventually come to accept that they cannot compete on the same playing field with most boys.

With puberty also comes breast development and the onset of menstruation. Some girls eagerly look forward to these changes, seeing them as portals to the mysterious world of adulthood. "I couldn't wait to start getting my periods," recalls one woman. "It seemed like that's when I'd become a grownup."

But for many girls, breasts become a source of discomfort and embarrassment, while menstruation brings a monthly reminder of feminine vulnerability. As Simone de Beauvoir explained:

> …puberty transforms the young girl's body. It is more
> fragile than formerly: the feminine organs are vulner-
> able, and delicate in their functioning: her strange
> and bothersome breasts are a burden, they remind
> her of their presence by quivering painfully during

> violent exercise…Menstruation is painful: headaches,
> overfatigue, abdominal pains, make normal activities
> distressing.[8]

Even today, in the aftermath of the women's movement that exploded in the 1960s, puberty continues to be a time of anxiety and confusion for most girls. The ego-deflating recognition of superior male strength and the self-consciousness induced by our own physiological changes coincide with a blossoming awareness of ourselves as sexual beings. Suddenly, it is not enough to be merely pretty. To reach the ultimate in feminine achievement, we must also be sexy. This can be even more complicated and even traumatic if we are starting to have questions about our sexual identity at this critical time in our development. For some girls, awareness of a preference for other girls can come early and, depending on family and community acceptance or rejection of GLBT lifestyles, our sexuality and what it means to be sexy can be especially confusing and anxiety-provoking.

Be Nice, but Be Sexy

Sex appeal is as old as humanity itself. Stone Age fertility goddesses, biblical temptresses, and mythical Sirens attest to the mysterious female power to attract and enthrall. As girls, we glimpse that power when we observe how boys and men respond to certain females.

When I was in fifth grade, one of my classmates dressed in short, tight skirts and crisp, white shirts or form-fitting sweaters. Our teacher, a male, said to her one day, "They sure didn't make girls like you when I was in fifth grade." His admiration was unmistakable and, for me, unsettling. I was still a jump-rope, hopscotch kind of girl whose idea of companionship was to bury myself in a book. Was I inferior to my classmate? Would my teacher—or for that matter, my peers—like me better if I tried to look like her?

Around this time I also began to hear snatches of whispered conversations about kissing and "necking" at parties where parents weren't present. The conversations were usually full of giggles and knowing looks, suggesting a world in which boys and girls did unimaginable things with each other.

Today's young women tend to be less naive than I was because they are exposed to overt sexuality at a much younger age. Websites, television programs, movies, music videos, and the fashion industry deliver the persistent and unavoidable message that to look good, girls have to look sexy. Furthermore, the purveyors of entertainment and fashion insist that sexiness is the key to a fulfilling life. Countless commercials and web and magazine ads depict beautiful, sexy young women desired by men, envied by their peers, and brimming with happiness that comes primarily from being sexually attractive. Girls absorb the message and measure themselves against the sex icons of pop culture.

But sex appeal goes beyond appearance, as girls soon learn. To make themselves more appealing to the opposite sex, even though we're more aware of societal conditioning, many begin to conform to the stereotypical feminine attributes of passivity and submissiveness. Girls may downplay their intelligence to avoid competing with boys, claiming that they just aren't good at math and science—areas associated with typically masculine career choices. They may feign weakness or lack of skill in something they are good at. One young woman I know is an excellent chess player, but she confessed that she never tries to beat her boyfriend at the game because it would hurt his ego. Although it has become more acceptable today to encourage girls to follow their talents and some of the old, limiting stereotypes are losing their power, many girls still tend to show deference to boys. I still see it consistently in the classes I teach in a community college: place one male with several women in a group project and, more often than not, the women will choose him to speak for the group, regardless of his ability or academic standing.

Research has also shown that by late adolescence, many girls become less willing to assert themselves, less willing to state honestly what they believe to be true. Psychologists attribute this reticence to a loss of self-confidence related to the physical and psychological upheaval of adolescence. And there's also an element of calculation, as girls try to transform themselves into an object of desire.

For, as most girls learn early on, sexiness is a path to female power. The late film actress Marilyn Monroe had an unstable childhood that included long stretches in foster care, but as a teenager she learned that wearing tight sweaters would attract male attention and the approval she craved. Reality TV star Kim Kardashian has earned millions of dollars by marketing her sexuality. And high school girls everywhere see their pretty, sexy peers often getting preferential treatment from their teachers and adulation from the boys.

But many girls are anxious and confused by the message that sexuality confers power. Our culture expects women to be "nice," and overt sexiness clashes with that expectation. As adolescents, we fear that we'll be scorned if we're a "prude" or "frigid," but we'll earn contempt if we're "easy." We feel the sting of being treated like an object, knowing that our human worth is diminished in the process, and we're offended by masculine leers and suggestive comments. Yet we are perturbed and our vanity is injured if we fail to attract male admiration. Many of us struggle to reconcile these puzzling, contradictory feelings well beyond adolescence.

The Prince Charming Myth

Along with the anxiety and confusion created by our budding sexuality, our sexual awakening is inevitably entangled with the fairy tales that have fed our imaginations since the cradle—the handsome prince falls in love with the beautiful maiden and bestows on her the gift of "happily ever after."

It is a story that has endured in innumerable forms for generations because it touches some deep longing within us. When Kate Middleton married Prince William, who made her a princess and future queen, she became the real-life version of the fairy tale almost every little girl had ever believed in. That she was the living embodiment of idealized femininity—pretty, submissive, kind, and sexy (in a nice way)—added luster to the story and instantly made her one of the most admired women in the world.

Whatever her inner struggles and insecurities may be, the Duchess of Cambridge projects an image of traditional womanhood embellished by modern glamour. Her life story is a new interpretation of the old fairy-tale myth that if we are nice enough, pretty enough, desirable enough, perfect enough, we will be rewarded with security, happiness, and love.

The myth, told and retold over the years, is absorbed into our subconscious as little girls, when doting family members call us "princess" and dress us up like dolls. If the myth is allowed to take root and blossom unexamined and unchallenged, it creates unrealistic expectations and encourages a level of passivity based on the notion that someone else is responsible for our happiness.

In this way, the prince charming myth paves the way for perpetual disappointment with ourselves, our romantic partners, and our lives—for the happiness and security we desire cannot be conferred on us by anyone. Instead, we must earn them through the arduous process of growing up.

WHO DO YOU THINK YOU ARE?

As we enter young adulthood, we have likely acquired some deeply rooted notions about our personal qualities and our place in the world. We have also developed a set of expectations about how other people will respond to us, as well as a repertoire of behaviors intended to attract approval, minimize distress, and avoid rejection.

These notions and behaviors stem from what we have been told and experienced repeatedly over our formative years. Our family, peers, and authority figures all contribute to our understanding of who we are. Societal expectations make an impact as well.

But are our beliefs about ourselves accurate, or are they a misreading of what has happened to us?

As children, we all encounter rejection, disappointment, loss, disillusionment, and failure to one degree or another. Negative experiences are part of the human condition, and no one is immune from pain. If we are lucky, we have support and guidance from people who love us and who can help us develop the emotional fortitude to withstand difficult circumstances. We also have positive experiences to counter the negative—such as recognition for our abilities, affirmation from friends, or the discovery of special interests that enhance the quality of our life.

And if we are very lucky, the cumulative weight of the positive exceeds that of the negative, letting us enter adulthood with a sense of ourselves as capable, worthwhile people—not perfect people, for we all have limitations and insecurities—but people with an emotional foundation sturdy enough to support the building of a satisfying life.

But if our negative experiences outweigh the positive—if our primary attachment was insecure, if we learned to see ourselves as outcasts among our peers, if we failed to conform to conventional gender expectations, if we had few chances to develop our talents and strengths, if there were no one to help us deal with our pain—we may enter adulthood with a fundamental sense of inadequacy.

Because as children we always tend to blame ourselves when bad things happen to us, the repeated battering of our sense of self may lead us to see ourselves as incompetent, unworthy, and unlovable.

And if our experiences have included trauma, our already low self-esteem may be shattered. In the next chapter, we will look at the far-reaching impact of trauma and how it damages our sense of self.

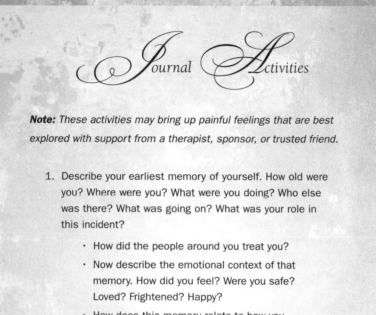

Journal Activities

Note: *These activities may bring up painful feelings that are best explored with support from a therapist, sponsor, or trusted friend.*

1. Describe your earliest memory of yourself. How old were you? Where were you? What were you doing? Who else was there? What was going on? What was your role in this incident?

   - How did the people around you treat you?
   - Now describe the emotional context of that memory. How did you feel? Were you safe? Loved? Frightened? Happy?
   - How does this memory relate to how you thought about yourself when you were a child? Was it typical, or does it stand out because it was different?

2. Remember yourself at a troubled time in your childhood. How old were you? What did you look like? Where were you? What was going on? How did you feel? Who else was involved?

   - Who was there to help you?
   - What did you wish would happen?
   - What actually happened?
   - How did this experience affect the way you thought about yourself?
   - How would you interpret this experience differently today?

3. How did you fit in with your childhood peers? How did other kids treat you? Were you part of a group? What was that group like?

   - What conclusions about yourself did you draw from the way other kids treated you?
   - What different conclusions could you draw today?

4. As a teenager, how did you experience your budding sexuality? Did you use sexuality to try to get what you wanted? Were you frightened of it? Confused by it? Did you try not to think about it? Was it not much of a factor in your life at that time?

   - Describe someone you were attracted to as a teenager. What was it about him or her that you liked?
   - What does that attraction say about how you felt about yourself?
   - What does that attraction say about what you wanted or needed from a romantic partner?
   - To what extent have those wants and needs changed over time?

5. Think of how you perceived yourself as you entered young adulthood. List ten words that describe how you thought of yourself at the time.

6. Today, how would you describe yourself as a young adult? Why?

2

TRAUMA AND THE DAMAGED SELF

Self-esteem isn't everything;
it's just that there's nothing without it.

—GLORIA STEINEM,
feminist, activist, and writer

Linda has an early memory of sitting in a high chair in a "poopy diaper." "My mother was there, and I remember being scared and ashamed," she says.

She doesn't remember what happened next, but she knows that fear and shame came to dominate her relationship with her mother. "She was very abusive, emotionally and physically," recalls Linda. "She always tore me down, always told me I was stupid and fat. She would start screaming at me, ranting and raving for fifteen or twenty minutes for the smallest thing—if I didn't vacuum right, if I didn't do the laundry right. One time she took off her high-heeled shoe and started hitting me with it. There was blood all over, on the wall, on the curtain."

Linda pauses to collect her thoughts. A small business owner who is active in Twelve Step programs for food and alcohol addictions, she chooses her words carefully. "I know now that my mother was addicted to prescription drugs and had a personality disorder. She was very narcissistic. But it took years for me to understand that. So I internalized all her abuse. I always thought there was something wrong with me. I was filled with guilt and shame."

Linda's relationship with her mother was unhealthy by any measure. But it went beyond that. Instead of providing the nurturing and security she needed as a little girl, Linda's world was chaotic and unpredictable. Any small event could set off a round of abuse. She was traumatized by repeated rejection, condemnation, and rage.

To numb her distress, Linda began to develop compulsive behaviors. "I started overeating when I was twelve," she recalls, "and I got made fun of at school because of my weight. So I started taking diet pills when I was fourteen. Then I started drinking to come down from the diet pills."

By her midteens, she had multiple addictions—to food, pills, alcohol, and pot. They masked her pain but also fed her sense of shame and worthlessness. The more she used, the worse she felt. The worse she felt, the more she used. Her weight fluctuated by a hundred pounds or more from year to year as she cycled through periods of bingeing and starving. She tried to keep her drinking hidden, but her husband and children weren't fooled.

"All those years, I hated myself. I thought my mother was right, that I was a worthless person," she says.

Finally, when her daughter confronted her about her drinking, Linda decided to get help. But it wasn't until she had done the hard work of psychotherapy and Twelve Step programs that she began to see the link between her compulsive behaviors and childhood trauma.

Trauma has a deep and lasting impact on our self-image and how we interact with the world. Even if we believe we have moved on, or we tell ourselves "it wasn't that bad," trauma stays deep in our subconscious memory, filling us with feelings of fear, helplessness, and shame. It is a hidden trigger behind our most damaging thoughts and emotions.

To fully appreciate trauma's far-reaching consequences, we must first understand what trauma is and how our minds and bodies respond to it.

THE TRAUMATIZED SELF

Not every bad thing that happens to us is traumatic. We all feel some degree of fear, stress, and sorrow at various times during our formative years. In our family, we may encounter conflict, betrayal, or an upsetting change of circumstances caused by a parent's job loss, illness, or divorce. At school, we may lose friends, do poorly in some subjects, or get taunted because of some physical or personality trait.

These and many other negative experiences are painful. They cause anxiety and sadness and sometimes a sense of loss that stays with us for years. But they do not necessarily cause trauma.

Psychological trauma is a deep, emotional wound caused by a stressful event or ongoing events in which we feel overwhelmed, fearful, and helpless. It can result from many things, including an unstable home environment; domestic violence; separation from a parent; serious illness or injury; bullying; neglect; and sexual, physical, or verbal abuse.

The event's severity isn't what matters—we don't have to face death or physical injury to be traumatized. It's our emotional response to an event that makes it traumatic. The more overwhelmed, frightened, and helpless we feel, the more likely we will be traumatized.

Trauma can occur at any stage of life. But because we are at our most helpless as children, we are more vulnerable to trauma during our formative years.

Take Linda, for example. As a child, she was the object of her mother's ongoing rage. Utterly dependent on her mother for the necessities of life, overwhelmed and frightened by the scope of her mother's anger, and powerless to change her situation, Linda was traumatized by her mother's attacks. To make matters worse, she internalized her mother's relentless message that she was a worthless human being.

For Johanie, the trauma happened in a different way. A professional pet groomer who's in recovery from alcohol and cocaine addiction, she recalls, "I had a pretty happy childhood until I was six or seven. My mom was kind of strict, but I knew she loved me. And my father adored me. I was his princess. He used to take me everywhere with him. But something happened and my mom and dad started fighting all the time. They'd get drunk and have these horrible fights and call each other names and my mom would scream at the top of her lungs. It was like she was crazy."

Johanie pauses to catch her breath. The memories still upset her. "Sometimes they'd hit each other. One time she broke his glasses. Another time he gave her a black eye. I'd be in my bedroom listening to everything and absolutely shaking with terror. I couldn't understand why they would do that. I thought it was my fault."

She attempts a weak smile. "Then, when I was eleven, my dad left. He left my mom for some teenager. I didn't blame him. I hated my mom by then. I blamed her for driving him away. And I blamed myself. I wanted to go and live with him, but he wouldn't let me. I thought there was something wrong with me because he didn't want me anymore. So I started hating myself."

Johanie shakes her head. "He'd visit me once in a while at first, but then he stopped coming. So then it was just me and my mom, and I hated her for everything that happened. But I hated myself even more." She adds, "I haven't seen my dad in fifteen years, and he only lives a half hour away."

Although her parents' anger was not directed at her, Johanie was nevertheless traumatized by their behavior. Their frequent ugly fights shook her world. Her home, once secure and nurturing, had become a frightening place in which terrible things could happen without warning. She couldn't turn to her parents to soothe her distress because they were causing her distress. And when her father abandoned her, the last wall of her safe childhood world came crashing down.

Overwhelmed, frightened, and powerless to change the situation, Johanie—who had once enjoyed a secure childhood—suffered a traumatic psychological injury. Like Linda, her trauma was intensified by self-hatred.

Grace, who left school in the eighth grade and developed multiple addictions, is now in her early forties and earning a master's degree in psychology. But her youth was a succession of traumatic events. "We always had to look good on the outside," she recalls. "We'd get all dressed up for Sunday dinner, Mom was fixing a turkey, and the next thing you knew somebody had thrown the turkey out the window and people would be screaming. And I'd think, *But we were just at church a couple hours ago.* The contradiction always bothered me.'"

The clash between appearance and reality became even more upsetting when an uncle started molesting her. "When I finally got up the courage to tell my mother, she told me I was lying," says Grace. "She said I was making it up and just trying to cause trouble."

So the abuse continued, and Grace started acting out until her mother "had had enough." Grace explains, "My parents were divorced. One day she dropped me off at a Chinese restaurant and didn't tell me my dad was taking me home with him from there. Without even letting me know, she'd decided I was going to go live with him."

Grace ran away when she was thirteen. She was sent to a reformatory school where the punishment for bad behavior was to stay in a "time-out box"—a wooden cage in the basement where uncooperative students were held for forty-eight hours. Grace often ended up there.

"When I told my dad, he got me out, but from then on I pretty much lived from house to house, sometimes in abandoned buildings and stuff," says Grace. "I remember calling my mom one time and saying I hadn't eaten in a couple of days, could I come home. And she said 'Nope. You made your bed. You have to lie in it.'"

Grace learned to put on a tough exterior and survived as best she could. Her chaotic household and sexual abuse, her parents' rejection, her incarceration and homelessness—she stuffed all that trauma down into the deepest recesses of her being. But the damage was done, and the trauma—as it always does until it is addressed and healed—would have terrible consequences in her life for years.

What's most damaging about trauma is not the event or the

ongoing events themselves. We can survive those. It's that trauma
causes significant, lasting damage to our psychological development.

One of the tasks of growing up is to learn how to cope with adver-
sity, how to keep engaging with the world in a healthy way *despite*
the inevitable difficulties of life. In the process of facing problems,
finding solutions, and learning from mistakes, we begin to develop
an awareness of our likes and dislikes, our strengths and liabilities,
our goals and values. As we work through challenges, we begin to
discover who we are.

When we are severely traumatized, we can't do that effectively.
The psychic wound is so deep that it derails our emotional growth.
We see the world as a frightening, unpredictable place and ourselves
as vulnerable and helpless in the face of peril.

Because we could not control or change the traumatic events in
our life, we may start to believe we have no control over *any* aspect of
our lives—that nothing we do can make things better. Psychologists
call this "learned helplessness." Women who have incorporated this
belief into their identity feel powerless to chart the course of their
own lives. They believe that it would be futile to even try. In her book
Trauma and Addiction, Dr. Tian Dayton describes learned helplessness
as "a condition in which they [trauma victims] lose the capacity to
appreciate the connection between their actions and their ability to
influence their lives."[9]

When we are convinced that we are powerless to change anything
and that nothing we do matters, we are likely to give up before we
even start. This attitude keeps us stuck in unhealthy, unhappy situations and prevents us from trying to solve problems—the foundation of personal growth. What matters isn't our ability to actually *fix*
things, for there are lessons to be learned even from failure. It's our
ability to *try* that enables us to learn and build self-esteem. Learned
helplessness interferes with this process.

Another damaging legacy of childhood trauma is shame. It is
human nature to look for the reasons behind events, to understand

why something happened. Unfortunately, children usually blame themselves when bad things happen. In the words of psychologist Angie Panos:

> As children we tend to blame ourselves for things that happen around us, because we are limited in our capacity to think about others being responsible. In a five-year-old's mind if something bad happened, then she or he must have deserved it; therefore the universe makes sense. It is not until around age 12 that we gain the cognitive capacity to see how others' actions and behaviors are more complex with varying degrees of culpability. However, there are many confusing messages about responsibility in our culture, causing even adult victims of trauma confusion over responsibility for the perpetrator's actions.[10]

It makes sense to examine our own choices and actions when bad things happen to us. That's how we can recognize the part we played in a negative experience and avoid repeating mistakes. But trauma victims tend to take *all* the blame for negative events. The fear, helplessness, and shame at their core lead them to conclude that bad things happen to them because they are bad people.

As Dr. Panos puts it, "Shame can . . . leave victims of trauma feeling different and less worthy and in some cases even bad or evil themselves . . . causing greater intensity in the psychological wounds. The end result is that a traumatized person no longer feels worthy of being loved, accepted, and having good things happen to them in their life."[11]

So, while unhealed childhood trauma stunts our emotional growth, our learned helpnessness and our shame cramp that growth even more. We come to believe that we lack the capacity to improve our lot in life—and that we don't deserve better, anyway. Fear, pain, and shame fill the core of our being, where our fragile sense of self is repeatedly assaulted by self-doubt and self-rejection.

What a painful way to live—to believe that there is no hope for a better life and that we are not worthy of anything better!

In time, the pain and inner turmoil of unhealed trauma can lead to emotional disorders that further limit our ability to create a satisfying life. Research has consistently shown that childhood trauma greatly increases the risk of developing adult depression, anxiety disorders, behavioral addictions, and addictions to alcohol and other drugs. An article published in 2007 by the National Institutes of Health noted:

> Research suggests that PTEs [potentially traumatic expe-
> riences] experienced in childhood are associated with
> a greater degree of psychopathology than trauma first
> experienced in adulthood. For instance, in a commu-
> nity population, those who were sexually assaulted in
> childhood were more likely than those first assaulted in
> adulthood to report subsequent major depression, drug
> and alcohol use disorders, and phobias . . . In another
> community-based study of adult women, women with
> a history of childhood abuse were more likely to exhibit
> symptoms of depression and anxiety as compared with
> those who were victims of assault in adulthood.[12]

Of course, not all trauma results in emotional disorders, just as not all emotional disorders stem from trauma. We are born with genetic predispositions to a whole host of physical and psychological strengths and weaknesses, including tendencies toward emotional disorders and addictions. When environmental factors such as trauma and stress interact with our genetically inherited vulnerabilities, our mental health is almost certain to suffer.

Research has also shown that women are more vulnerable to depression than men. A 2009 article published by Frontiers in Behavioral Neuroscience discussed the combined influences of stress, genetics, and gender on the development of depression:

In addition to the role of stress and genetic factors, there are important sex differences in the risk to develop depression. Major depression is twice as common in women as in men . . . Moreover, women more frequently develop depression in response to childhood trauma compared to men . . . Sex differences in the risk for stress-related depression have been hypothesized to be, in part, due to direct effects of circulating estrogens . . . Taken together, it appears that a complex interaction between several intrinsic factors, i.e. genes and sex, and stressful experience underlie depression risk in most cases. [13]

These researchers and many others have concluded that our genetic inheritance and childhood experiences play an important role in shaping our mental health. Furthermore, the fact that we are female increases our risk of depression. If we are living with unhealed childhood trauma, scientists say, we are more prone to depression, anxiety, and other emotional problems as an adult.

Although we may come to believe that our mental health issues are unrelated to trauma—we may tell ourselves that "I'm just made this way"—our emotional difficulties are often a sign of our inner pain.

How Self-Defense Becomes Self-Harm

For people with a relatively healthy sense of self, coping with trauma typically unfolds in three stages: protest, numbing, and mourning. At first, we may express anger, become verbally abusive, or act out in self-destructive or hostile ways. In this protest phase, our moods may swing widely, and we may be unusually irritable and short-tempered. Then comes numbing, a deadening of our emotions and a feeling of disconnectedness. We may withdraw from our environment and isolate ourselves from others. Finally, we may need to mourn. Whatever the cause of our trauma, we have lost something precious—our sense of the world as a safe place—and we must grieve our loss.

These reactions can last from a few days to many months as our mind processes the trauma. Gradually, the impact of the traumatic event fades. But trauma victims often feel painful emotions from time to time long after the event, especially when something—a sound, a smell, an anniversary date—reminds them of what happened.

For many of us, however, the healing process isn't a matter of days or months. In fact, the trauma is not healed at all. Instead, we absorb it into our psyche, where it merges with our core sense of self. We view everything and everyone through the distorting lens of trauma.

We may pretend that it isn't there or that it no longer hurts. We may tell ourselves that we're over it. But trauma stays deep in our subconscious, where it becomes a festering source of damaging thoughts and painful emotions. If we look back at the traumatic episode and consider its impact, we may see two selves: the person we were before it happened, and the fearful, shame-filled person we became afterwards.

When trauma becomes part of our core being, we may subconsciously develop defensive strategies meant to protect us from pain. But in fact, these strategies keep us stuck in the trauma. Let's look at the three broad types of defensive strategies: shutting down, behavioral addictions, and substance addictions.

Shutting Down

We shut down when we build walls around ourselves that keep us from connecting with other people in meaningful ways. As women, we tend to experience the world emotionally, and interpersonal relationships are key to our sense of well-being. But when we've been traumatized, we may find ourselves unable to let others get close to us. We may choose the safety of isolation over the risk of vulnerability.

I, myself, became an expert at building walls. Shamed and hurt by my peers' rejection, I believed that something was basically wrong with me and that nobody would ever like me. To avoid the pain of further rejection, I became a loner. As a young adult I avoided social situations, ignored any overtures of friendship, buried my nose in a book in the lunchroom at work, and went on long walks by myself for recreation. That way, I never had to risk re-experiencing my most painful memories: the anguish of walking through the schoolyard and being spit on, the humiliation of my surprise tenth birthday party to which nobody came, the devastation of walking into a school cafeteria and freezing in the face of thundering jeers.

The invisible wall I built around myself made me lonely and sad, but it was my defense against the even greater pain of rejection and shame. Other women may shut down in less obvious ways. Some may adopt an attitude of rigid independence—"I don't need anyone! I can do it all myself." Others may keep their romantic partner and friends at an emotional distance.

One woman in a Twelve Step meeting told the group, "I wouldn't let anyone know the real me. I didn't even know who the real me was. So I was always faking it. I was always trying to be what I thought people wanted me to be. I thought if I tried to act like them, they'd accept me, but if they knew the real me they wouldn't like me. So I was acting all the time."

Building genuine relationships requires us to be vulnerable, to risk exposing our inner world, flaws and all. When we shut down, we can't fully experience the healing power of connection because we're so afraid of getting hurt that we never let anyone close to us. Our relationships, such as they are, are built on a foundation of pretense and mistrust.

Behavioral Addictions

Also called process addictions, behavioral addictions offer another way to avoid the pain of our unhealed trauma: we compulsively behave certain ways despite serious negative consequences to our well-being. The many areas of potential behavioral addictions

include food (starving or bingeing), sex, gambling, shopping, shoplifting, pornography, video games, work, exercise, Internet surfing,
and cutting.

Whatever the addiction, the behavior helps us escape our inner
turmoil first, by distracting us from our core pain, and second, by
triggering the release of pleasure-producing chemicals in our brain.

The brain's reward center—a circuit of chemical messengers and
electrical impulses—gives us the ability to feel happiness. When we
eat a good meal, have satisfying sex, or engage in other fulfilling
activities, our reward center releases dopamine, endorphins, and
other *neurotransmitter* chemicals that carry messages of pleasure,
calm, and euphoria. (The brain also has neurotransmitters for messages of pain, fear, anger, and so on.) The chemical messengers then
connect with targeted receptors in the brain that fire off a pleasurable
sensation.

From an evolutionary viewpoint, our reward center promotes
behaviors that help our species survive (eating, procreating, and
social bonding). It also eases physical suffering. When we talk of a
"runner's high" or "endorphin rush," we are referring to the feeling
of well-being and exhilaration that can follow an episode of pain,
danger, or stress. Most of us who have experienced the ordeal of
childbirth, for example, have also felt the profound well-being that
floods our body soon afterward.

Unfortunately, our brain releases its "feel-good" chemicals even
when we take healthy behaviors to unhealthy extremes, or we
endanger ourselves through high-risk activities such as gambling,
shoplifting, or promiscuous sex. Our body's own chemicals reinforce
the compulsive behaviors intended to distract us from our core pain.

Linda, for example, discovered in food a profound source of
pleasure. "Somehow, as a little girl I found that whenever I felt sad
or anxious or afraid, I could make myself feel better by eating," she
recalls. Of course, eating provided only temporary relief, so she constantly had to eat more to calm her inner turmoil. It seemed as if she

could never have enough. Then, as the weight piled on, she resorted to starving herself.

"I did a lot of bingeing and starving," she says. "Even though I was deeply ashamed of my behavior, I couldn't stop." Food—whether she was consuming it or avoiding it—became a major distraction and source of comfort.

Carol says that in her battle to stay thin, she adhered to a strict eating regimen with "almost manic vigilance and self-control"—and the effort gave her the illusion of control over a life filled with inner turmoil.

Johanie turned to sex to escape the pain of her traumatic childhood. "Maybe it had something to do with my dad walking out on me. I don't know," she says wistfully. "I just remember being in bars and feeling lonely and awful about myself, and then I'd catch some guy's eyes and there'd be this flood of excitement. And my heart would start pounding and I'd get all tingly and shaky. It was like the most wonderful thing in the world was about to happen."

Johanie estimates that she had sex with more than a hundred guys, most of them one-night stands. "It wasn't about the sex," she says. "That part didn't matter to me. I mean, I'd pretend to be all turned on and everything. But it was just going through the motions. What I got addicted to was that moment when you look in their eyes and you know what's going to happen but it hasn't happened yet. It was exciting. The only time I felt really alive was when I was picking up some guy."

My friend Meg was a cutter in her teens. Looking back on it, she explains, "What I remember is being terrified that I was destined to always be alone—I was going to grow into a woman that nobody would ever want, that I was unlovable. I cried myself to sleep almost every night. But for some reason, cutting myself made me feel better."

She repeatedly cut the skin on her inner arms—leaving inch-long stripes of beaded blood—and wore long sleeves to hide the evidence. When her mother finally noticed, she started cutting herself on her thighs and stomach where no one would see it. The behavior lasted almost two years. "I wasn't trying to kill myself. It wasn't that. It was just that the physical pain seemed to make me feel better," she says.

And that's the point of behavioral addictions—they make us feel better by taking our attention away from our inner pain and triggering the release of soothing chemicals in our brain. But ultimately, even that brief relief further damages our already battered sense of self when we feel the shame and despair of not being able to control our destructive behaviors.

Substance Addictions

A third strategy for escaping the pain of unhealed childhood trauma is to use mood-altering substances. Research has consistently shown a strong link between childhood trauma and addiction, particularly in women. Some estimates say that as many as 85 percent of women with addictions experienced some form of childhood trauma: sexual abuse, physical abuse, emotional abuse, physical neglect, or witnessing violence. An article published by the National Institute on Alcohol Abuse and Alcoholism reported that, for women, the link between substance abuse and post-traumatic stress disorder (PTSD) is particularly strong. In fact, the risk is two to three times higher for females than males, with 30 to 57 percent of female substance abusers meeting the PTSD criteria. That risk, the study said, "is related to their higher incidence of childhood physical and sexual abuse."[14]

Although not all women with chemical addictions had unhappy or traumatic childhoods, many girls who become substance abusers experienced trauma during their formative years. For these young women—many of whom begin experimenting with drugs and alcohol when they are too young and naïve to foresee the calamity that addiction will bring—the discovery that substances can instantly take away pain and produce pleasure is life-altering.

The Chemical Cure

Like behavioral addictions, addictive substances work on the brain's reward center. But they do it even more directly and efficiently. They either mimic the brain's own pleasure messenger chemicals, or they overstimulate the reward center to release more of those chemicals.

Some drugs, such as marijuana and heroin, have a chemical structure that is similar to the structure of dopamine and endorphins. When these drugs enter the brain, they connect with receptors in the reward center just as their naturally occurring counterparts do. So we don't have to eat, have sex, listen to music, or engage in any other activity in order to experience a flood of pleasure. We can feel calm, content, and euphoric simply by shipping the counterfeit pleasure messenger chemicals to our brain.

Other drugs, such as cocaine and methamphetamine, trick our brain's reward center by making it release abnormally large amounts of neurotransmitters—primarily dopamine—or by stopping the normal recycling process in which neurotransmitters are re-absorbed by the brain. As a result, the brain is awash in dopamine and other pleasure messenger chemicals, producing feelings of energy, alertness, confidence, and an exaggerated sense of well-being.

Alcohol also stimulates the release of neurotransmitters, including dopamine and gamma-aminobutyric acid (GABA), which reduces anxiety and causes drowsiness. In the early stage of intoxication, we may feel unusually happy and lively. But as the GABA takes effect, we are likely to want only to sleep.

However the mood-altering chemicals achieve their effects, the process of becoming addicted is the same for almost everyone. At first, we use because it makes us feel good—so good, in fact, that we want to do it over and over again. But the more chemicals we send to our brain, the more our brain tries to achieve a balance. It does this by producing fewer pleasure neurotransmitters of its own or by reducing the number of receptors available for the chemicals to connect with.

As a result, dopamine and other pleasure neurotransmitters have a weaker impact on the reward center, and this in turn diminishes the "high." Not only is the pleasure of using diminished, the user's ability to enjoy *anything* is diminished because the brain's reward center is compromised. And, according to the National Institute on Drug Abuse (NIDA), this pattern "compels the addicted person to keep abusing drugs in an attempt to bring the dopamine function back to normal, except now larger amounts of the drug are required to achieve the same dopamine high—an effect known as tolerance."

NIDA also explains:

> Long-term abuse causes changes in other brain chemical
> systems and circuits as well . . . Brain imaging studies
> of drug-addicted individuals show changes in areas of
> the brain that are critical to judgment, decision making,
> learning and memory, and behavior control. Together,
> these changes can drive an abuser to seek out and take
> drugs compulsively despite adverse, even devastating
> consequences—that is the nature of addiction.[15]

As young women burdened by painful childhoods and trauma, Linda, Johanie, and Grace all discovered that chemical remedies provided almost instant relief—and all paid a terrible price for that discovery.

"I began sneaking vodka out of my parents' liquor cabinet when I was around thirteen," Linda recalls. "I knew immediately that this was something that could make me feel better. I'd put it in my orange juice and take it to school with me."

Johanie started smoking pot when she was fourteen. "I loved it instantly," she says. "I had this best friend whose father had also abandoned him and we'd get high together all the time. Just smoke and lie on the grass and look at the sky and laugh our asses off. It didn't matter about our dads. The pot made life beautiful."

During Grace's years as a homeless teenager, she drank and used drugs only when she was around other people who were using. At eighteen, she married an older man and had four children in quick succession. "I smoked pot and drank a little bit, but not much," she says of those years. "My husband was a Muslim, and I tried to be like him."

But the marriage fell apart. As her traumatic past and chaotic present collided, Grace felt overwhelmed and frightened. She found that alcohol and cocaine soothed her distress. Eventually, she was arrested for drug possession and stealing and was ordered into a twenty-eight-day treatment program. She stayed clean for eighteen months, until she relapsed and set in motion a destructive cycle that resulted in losing custody of her children.

Linda and Johanie also faced the destructive consequences of addiction. Alcohol seriously damaged Linda's family relationships and brought her to the brink of bankruptcy. Cocaine and alcohol addiction led Johanie to prostitution and jail.

Like most chemically dependent women, Linda, Johanie, and Grace were deeply ashamed of their substance abuse and of their inability to control their behavior. The more they used, the less they liked themselves. The less they liked themselves, the more they used. In this way, addiction trapped then into repeating over and over again the very trauma they were trying to escape.

The same can be said of all dysfunctional defensive strategies. When we build walls, develop behavioral addictions, get hooked on substances, or engage in other dysfunctional behaviors to escape our inner pain, we continually re-experience the central emotions of trauma and its aftermath: overwhelming fear, helplessness, and shame. In a very real sense, our lives come to revolve around the trauma that never goes away.

THE PHYSICAL IMPACT OF TRAUMA

Scientists have long known that stress is linked to heart disease, diabetes, asthma, hypertension, autoimmune diseases, and other serious ailments. More recently, scientists have found that the stress of child-hood trauma can damage our physical health well into adulthood.

Furthermore, the physical impact of trauma has a profound influ-ence on our emotions. Body and mind are intricately entwined.

"A wide spectrum of later disorders and symptoms have been linked to early-life stress and abuse, including cardiovascular disease, fibromyalgia, fatigue, anxiety, and addiction," said a 2010 article in the Association for Psychological Science's *Observer.* "Far from being transient, stress experienced early in life has long-term and damaging effects on the entire body."[16]

And medical imaging reveals that sexual abuse in childhood actu-ally changes the way girls' brains develop, said a 2012 Medscape Medical News report. The abuse leads to a "thinner somatosensory cortex"—the area of the brain that processes sensations related to touch—and "smaller hippocampal volume"— the region of the brain (the hippocampus) that processes and organizes information, creates memories, and governs concentration.[17] These changes are linked to mood and anxiety disorders, as well as to sexual anhedonia—the inability to feel sexual pleasure. In fact, sexual abuse survivors may find it hard to fully experience pleasure at all.

Lisa, now an athletic woman in her midforties, was abandoned by both parents as an infant. Between the ages of five and thirteen, she was repeatedly raped by teenage boys. "They were neighbors," she recalls. "Four or five of them would take me down to the basement. I don't remember a lot about it, except I can still see myself as this little girl with this guy on top of me. I didn't tell anyone because I was the bad person. When I was thirteen, my brother walked in and saw it. He told my grandmother and she must have done something, because it stopped after that."

Lisa relates the experience with no visible sign of emotion—with what her therapist describes as a flat affect: "I'm not emotional about it. I can't feel it," she explains.

But the damage was done, and her life spun out of control. Her school attendance became sporadic, she started getting into fights, and she began drinking alcoholically. "The first time I drank, I drank a six-pack of beer. I blacked out, puked, and couldn't wait to do it again."

She and her friends often found an older guy to buy alcohol for them. "We called it tapping a Harry," she says. "'Let's go tap a Harry.'"

By the time Lisa was eighteen, she had been arrested three times for driving under the influence and multiple times for assault and battery. Her life plan, such as it was, "was to become a heroin addict and die at twenty-one." She thought about suicide a lot. "If I wasn't drinking or drugging, I had to have another way out. The only way out for me was ending my life. It was always an option."

She was sent to a locked rehab facility, where she got sober for the first time. Today, after many years in recovery, Lisa admits, "I have a good life. But I still don't know what it really feels like to be happy, joyful, or free. I know the concept. But I can't feel it."

The inability to feel joy may be a direct consequence of structural changes to her brain. As a vulnerable little girl, those changes helped her block out the pain and memories of the abuse. But as an adult, she is working to undo the protective barriers so she can experience joy and happiness more fully.

Grace, too, is living with the legacy of childhood sexual abuse. She knows that the impact of trauma is both emotional and physical. "Memory is cellular," she explains. "It's carried in your entire body. I can be walking somewhere and smell a certain smell and I'm right back to the sexual abuse. Nauseous, sweaty, shaky. It's like it's happening all over again."

Johanie has had similar experiences with her own physical response to past trauma. "If I see a guy who's wearing a hat or holding his head a certain way that reminds me of my dad, I'll get this sick feeling in the pit of my stomach. Like this big knot."

Why does childhood trauma have such power? One reason is that traumatic memory is stored in the part of our brain that is linked with survival. It is here that the "fight-flight-freeze" response originates when we're faced with danger. When this response is activated, the sympathetic nervous system releases a flood of adrenalin and other hormones. Our heart races, we breathe faster, and our blood vessels dilate, automatically preparing us for extreme physical exertion.

In this state of high alert, sensory input becomes more intense. Sounds, smells, and images get burned into our brain. This is why we all remember where we were when something traumatic happened—like the 9/11 terror attacks, for instance. And it's why we recall one critical remark, ignoring a dozen compliments. When our automatic defense response is activated, we take note and remember.

Unfortunately, traumatic memory is stored without context. That is, instead of being remembered as an event with a beginning, middle, and end—as we remember a nice day at the beach, for example, or a favorite date—traumatic memory is stored as bits and pieces of something overwhelming and frightening and inexplicable. Then, when something reminds us of the past—a smell, a sound, an image—we link those fragmented memories to current events. In this way, we re-experience the traumatic event again and again. According to Dr. Tian Dayton:

> Events that a nontraumatized person might pass over or have only a temporary reaction to can send a previously traumatized person into an emotional tailspin that might include withdrawal, anger, belligerence, fear, hurt or rage. The traumatized person is reacting to a currently upsetting situation . . . with the intensity of feelings appropriate not to this situation but to the original trauma. They are getting triggered, stuck in yesterday, constantly reliving the cycle of intense feeling associated with the original traumatic episode or the cumulative trauma of an earlier pain-filled relationship.[18]

All of this happens on a subconscious level, where present and past are linked almost instantly. Our response is instantaneous as well, filling us with anxiety and throwing our body into the stress-response mode.

The fight-flight-freeze mechanism is a short-term state of physical arousal that enables us to survive immediate danger, after which we normally return to a balanced state. But subconscious memories can make us feel anxious, frightened, and overwhelmed much of the time, wreaking havoc not only on our emotions but on our physical health as well. Our body suffers as it struggles to cope with long-term unresolved stress—stress triggered by current events that repeatedly take us back to the traumatic past.

That's why "talk therapy" is so important in healing the damage of childhood trauma. When we talk about our trauma in the safe setting of a therapeutic relationship, we begin to bring it out of our subconscious memory. We start to think about it in new ways, to see it as an episode with a beginning, middle, and end—as something that happened *to* us, rather than something that *is* us. (The techniques of motivational enhancement or cognitive-behavioral therapy are especially helpful as we make those distinctions and draw on our own strengths.) And we begin to understand ourselves not as the helpless child we were, but as a maturing adult who is free to make choices about how we conduct our life.

Talking about our trauma is one of the most difficult things we will ever do. It lays bare the feelings we have tried so hard to run away from. It brings us face-to-face with our buried pain. Yet, until we summon the courage to face what we have tried so hard to run away from, we continually relive the trauma through other experiences and other relationships. And we continue to pay the price with our emotional and physical health.

Unfortunately for women with addictions, childhood trauma is not the only source of pain. Addiction itself is a trauma, an assault on the self. In the next chapter we will look at how addiction to substances sabotages our behaviors, distorts our thought processes, and disrupts our complicated journey toward adulthood.

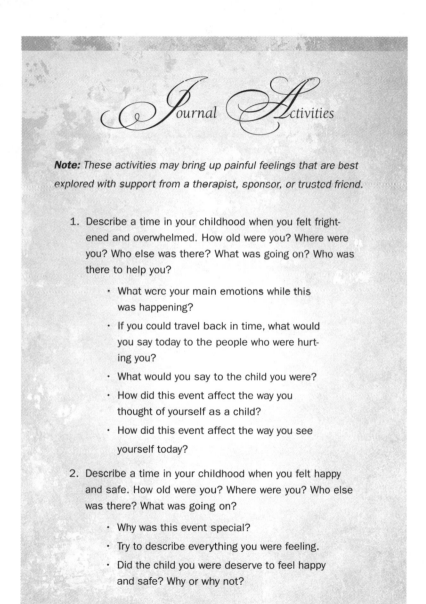

Journal Activities

Note: *These activities may bring up painful feelings that are best explored with support from a therapist, sponsor, or trusted friend.*

1. Describe a time in your childhood when you felt frightened and overwhelmed. How old were you? Where were you? Who else was there? What was going on? Who was there to help you?

   - What were your main emotions while this was happening?
   - If you could travel back in time, what would you say today to the people who were hurting you?
   - What would you say to the child you were?
   - How did this event affect the way you thought of yourself as a child?
   - How did this event affect the way you see yourself today?

2. Describe a time in your childhood when you felt happy and safe. How old were you? Where were you? Who else was there? What was going on?

   - Why was this event special?
   - Try to describe everything you were feeling.
   - Did the child you were deserve to feel happy and safe? Why or why not?

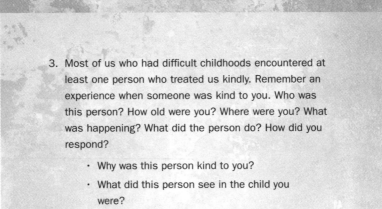

3. Most of us who had difficult childhoods encountered at
   least one person who treated us kindly. Remember an
   experience when someone was kind to you. Who was
   this person? How old were you? Where were you? What
   was happening? What did the person do? How did you
   respond?

   - Why was this person kind to you?
   - What did this person see in the child you
     were?
   - How did you feel after this experience?

4. Describe a time in your childhood or adolescence when
   you successfully dealt with a difficult situation. What was
   going on? How old were you? Where were you? What did
   you do? What was the outcome?

   - What inner strengths did this experience
     reveal about you?

5. How can you be kind to yourself today?

3

ADDICTION AND THE LOSS OF SELF

❧

Everybody kind of understands, oh yeah,
you take drugs and it does something to your
brain and then you can't stop. It's easier to
describe that shame, that horrible feeling of
not being able to control your own life.

—AIMEE MANN,
singer-songwriter

"The last time I drank, I hoped to drink myself to death," Marcela says with a catch in her voice. "I was broken down. I wanted to die."

She sits at her desk in a small office overflowing with books and papers and manila folders. Pictures of smiling women and children are tacked to a message board along with thank-you notes and phone numbers and meeting notices. It's here that she welcomes newcomers to the recovery house for women fresh out of detox—here that she herself arrived nearly three years ago when she was "sick of doing the same thing over and over again."

"I was desperate and miserable and angry at myself when I walked through that door," she recalls. "So I know how women feel when they come here. They're here because they have nothing left. They're broken inside."

She hesitates, then pulls a yellowed snapshot out of the desk drawer. It shows a gaunt, grim woman with angry eyes. "That was me," she says. I find it hard to see a resemblance between the face in the photo and the vibrant young woman sitting across from me.

"I keep it to remind myself what hopelessness feels like," she explains. "Because this place gave me hope, and that's what saved me. That's what I try to give to the women who come here. Hope."

Marcela's been a counselor at the home for almost two years. Before that, she worked as a nurse's aide, but she lost her job when her addiction to alcohol and prescription drugs took over her life. Her boyfriend wound up in jail, and with no way to support herself, she moved in with her mother.

"My mother's an amazing woman," Marcela says with pride. "She came over from Puerto Rico with nothing and built up a cleaning business all by herself. She bought her own house and raised four kids and always made sure we had good food and nice clothes. She's my hero."

Marcela's father stayed in Puerto Rico, but she and her siblings visited him and their extended family every year. "My parents get along fine. They aren't like some parents who are always fighting and trash-talking each other. But my dad has an eye for the ladies, and my mom got sick of it." She shrugs. "I don't blame her."

Marcela describes her childhood as happy and says she never doubted that her parents loved her. "My dad was a good father in his own way," she says. "I mean, I didn't come from this messed-up background or anything. I wasn't abused. But I became an addict anyway, and I did some shameful things."

Soon after she moved in with her mother, she started helping herself to cash from her mother's purse—"ten dollars here, twenty there," Marcela recalls. "That didn't go far, so then I started stealing things and pawning them. I tried to take things she wouldn't notice, old jewelry and stuff. I told myself I'd get a job and get everything back for her, but I didn't."

The stealing extended to other family members until they caught on and told her to stay away. So she broke into a neighbor's house and stole an expensive camera. "That's the first time I got arrested," says Marcela. "They let me off with probation, but by then my boyfriend was out of jail and we started stealing together. I got caught again and went to jail for six months."

When she got out, she tried to stay clean, but it didn't last. She did two more stints in jail. "For a long time I couldn't say this without crying," Marcela admits. "I broke my mom's heart."

The last time she got out, her mother wouldn't let her come home, and her boyfriend was living with another woman. "So I had no one," Marcela says. "No one and no place to go. So I came here." She shakes her head. "My mom taught us to have good morals, to be decent people. After all this time, I still don't know why I did those things. Why I became an addict. Why I was a thief. There's a lot of shame, you know?" She adds, "Some of the women who come here say they were born addicts. I think it's partly true. I think there's something inside us, and once it gets triggered, watch out."

Marcela is echoing what scientists have known for a long time: addiction has a biological basis. There's strong evidence that some of us are born with an inherited vulnerability to addiction, just as some of us are prone to cancer, heart disease, or other illnesses. Studies using brain-imaging techniques have shown that addicts and non-addicts process mood-altering substances differently, and addicts' brains have more difficulty with impulse control.

This doesn't mean that we are destined from birth to become addicts, and there's nothing we can do to avoid it. It simply means that if we're born with a genetic or neurological vulnerability to addiction and if we have experiences that promote the use of alcohol and other drugs, we are at a high risk of developing substance abuse problems.

Genetic and neurological vulnerability helps to explain why some people who experiment with alcohol and other drugs never get addicted, while others "fall in love" with substances and make getting high the center of their life. It also helps to explain why some people who grew up in secure and nurturing families may nevertheless succumb to addiction, while others with extremely difficult childhoods may not.

Biology and environment both contribute to the development of addiction, which since 1956 has been recognized as a disease by the American Medical Association and since 1960 by the American Psychiatric Association. Both associations stress that addiction is not a moral failing or evidence of weak willpower. Rather, it is a deadly, progressive disease that always gets worse unless something intervenes to stop it.

Like all diseases, addiction inflicts its damage in identifiable ways. While some maladies weaken our heart or our respiratory system, for example, substance abuse affects not only our body but also our brain's emotional and cognitive centers, subtly and insidiously changing the way we think and feel—in short, changing our very essence. Over time, addiction damages every aspect of our life, mind, body, and spirit: our relationships, our job, our financial security, and—most damaging of all—our self-worth.

Long after we put down our last drink, pill, or fix—long after our journey of recovery has begun—the fallout from addiction lingers like an aching, open wound in our soul. To understand the devastating impact of addiction on our sense of self, let's begin by looking at how addiction develops and how it affects the way we think, behave, and respond to the world.

A Cunning Disease

A former neighbor of mine once confided that the most frightening moment of her life was when she realized she was addicted to heroin. As a kid, she had been, in her words, "a born rebel," sneaking out of the house, smoking cigarettes, making out with boys. By the time she was twelve, she was smoking pot and drinking alcohol after school and on weekends. At fifteen, she started stealing pills out of friends' medicine cabinets. At seventeen, she developed a dependence on narcotic painkillers, which segued into a full-blown heroin addiction.

"I was always so willful, so headstrong," she said. "I thought I could get away with anything. But one morning I was sitting at the kitchen table sick as a dog, and I couldn't let my mom know why.

And all I kept thinking over and over was, 'I need a fix. I need a fix. I have to get a fix.' And there was this flash of shock, like I was about to fall over a cliff. Because I knew all of a sudden that I couldn't live without it. I was terrified."

For some women, the realization that they are addicted comes in a flash, in one brief, stunning moment of clarity. For others, the awareness emerges gradually—for example, the woman who routinely has a few drinks to unwind and finally begins to sense that she can't get through the day without alcohol. Whether the recognition of addiction is sudden or gradual, however, the process of becoming addicted follows a predictable pattern.

As we saw in chapter 2, all substances of abuse target the brain's reward center, the circuitry that releases and links "feel-good" chemicals in response to enjoyable activities or pain. When we take a sip of alcohol or a hit of marijuana—the substances we're most likely to try for the first time as adolescents or young women—the reward circuitry is activated and we experience a pleasurable sensation and a reduction of stress.

If we have had a reasonably nurturing childhood, suffered no unhealed trauma, and carry no genetic or neurological vulnerability to addiction, we may (or may not) enjoy using these substances. *But we will probably not feel compelled to continue using.* Alcohol, pot, and anything else we experiment with aren't likely to have a lasting impact on our priorities or on the way we conduct our life.

If, however, we are burdened by a difficult childhood, unhealed trauma, depression or other mental health issues, or were born with a genetic or neurological vulnerability to addiction—and especially if we have some combination of these factors—there's a strong chance that our early experimentation with alcohol and other drugs will alter the course of our lives.

Many women who go on to develop addictions say that their first exposure to mood-altering substances was like falling in love—"the best feeling in the world" or "what I was waiting for all my life." It was so wonderful, in fact, that they wanted to do it over and over again. Before long, they could think of little else.

It is in the need, the *compulsion* to use that the seeds of addiction are sown. For the budding addict, other pleasures and other activities gradually take a backseat to the increasingly urgent drive to get and use substances. As Marcela put it, "I used to think about drinking all the time. It was always in my head, you know, when I was going to buy it, where I was going to drink it, how I was going to hide it. And once I took a drink, I couldn't stop. I always had to have more until I passed out."

As alcohol and other drugs consume more time and attention, other pursuits fall by the wayside: school, work, recreation, goals, family, and non-using friends. The developing addict is increasingly motivated by just one thing: to re-experience the incredible pleasure of her early chemical highs. Her obsessive focus on substances is to some extent a conscious choice. But, more ominously, it also reflects the physiological changes taking place deep within her brain.

When experimentation with substances evolves into regular use, the brain's reward center begins to adjust. To ward off the unnatural state of being awash in dopamine, endorphins, and other pleasure-related chemicals, the brain tries to strike a balance by reducing its normal production of these chemicals. As a result, the artificial substances are now less effective, and the emerging addict must increase her use in an attempt to achieve the high she is seeking.

This condition is known as *tolerance,* a sign that the brain has begun to rely on artificial chemicals. As the brain produces fewer and fewer pleasure-related chemicals of its own, greater quantities of alcohol and other drugs must be consumed—not to feel high, but simply to feel normal. "I need alcohol to function" (or cocaine, or oxy, or heroin, or meth...)—that's what women say when their brains have been conditioned to rely on mood-altering chemicals.

To make matters worse, when the chemicals are not present, the brain becomes distressed and the user goes into *withdrawal.*

Withdrawal occurs in two stages: *acute* symptoms that typically last from a few days to a couple of weeks, and *chronic* symptoms that can last for many months as the brain resets its chemical balance.

In the acute stage, symptoms tend to be the exact opposite of the effects produced by the substances themselves. For example, withdrawal from stimulants, such as amphetamines and cocaine, generally induces an immediate crash—a period of intense depression and fatigue. On the other hand, people who take opiates for their calming and pain-easing effects have different withdrawal symptoms when they stop: nausea, chills, muscle and bone pain, and agitation. Alcohol, a depressant that initially acts as a stimulant by lowering inhibitions, causes withdrawal symptoms similar to those associated with both stimulants and opiates.

As unpleasant as acute withdrawal is, chronic (long-term) withdrawal presents an even greater obstacle to abstinence. Over the many months that it can take for the brain to repair itself and re-establish its natural chemical balance, women trying to get sober must cope with a host of distressing physical and psychological challenges. These can include aches and pains, digestive problems, irritability, and severe insomnia. One woman who was addicted to benzodiazepines reported that even after nine months in recovery, her skin still felt raw, like it was "all nerve endings."

For many women, one of the most troubling aspects of early sobriety is the inability to sleep—a direct result of the effects of alcohol and other drugs. Normal sleep patterns involve the interaction of many neurotransmitters, including dopamine, which plays a key role in regulating brain activity during sleep. Substances of abuse severely deplete the dopamine in the brain's reward center and can lead to chronic insomnia.

More than an inconvenience, sleep deprivation can cause serious health problems. It compromises the central nervous system, cardiovascular system, and immune system and can lead to depression, racing thoughts, agitation, exhaustion, and poor decision-making—all of which increase the stress of early abstinence.

But physical and psychological turmoil aren't the only factors that make it hard for a woman to abstain from substances once her brain has become accustomed to them. Amidst the misery of withdrawal, her chemical-starved brain generates powerful, persistent cravings that remind her of the instant pleasure and relief that alcohol and other drugs can deliver.

Now the cycle of addiction is in full swing: the addicted woman feels pleasure and relief when she drinks or uses drugs; she feels pain and suffering when their effects wear off; her brain demands its chemical remedy; and so she uses again. Without fully understanding what has happened to her, the woman—or, more and more commonly, the girl—who began by experimenting has become addicted. Her life is now largely defined by the most basic of human impulses: the desire to experience pleasure and avoid pain.

Now let's pause and consider the far-reaching impact of this development on the young woman's sense of self. Her nonaddicted peers have the potential to go to school, pursue careers, develop their talents, make new friends, create healthy relationships, work through disappointment and failure, and build resilience. In short, young women who are not addicted have the potential to face the challenges of growing up, building self-knowledge and self-esteem in the process.

The young woman who has become addicted, however, will have far fewer opportunities to mature. She may try to go to school, start a career, or build relationships, but her efforts will be sabotaged by the cycle of using, withdrawal, and cravings that has become her focal point. She devotes most of her energy to getting and using substances. When she faces obstacles and disappointment, when she feels unhappy or anxious, she will resort to chemicals to make herself feel better, rather than trying to work things through.

When we stop facing life's challenges and instead take the chemical escape, we stop doing the hard work of growing up. That's why it is said in Twelve Step meetings that we stop maturing at the age we start abusing substances. The thirty-year-old who got addicted at fourteen is still fourteen, emotionally and psychologically. Or, as Carolyn Knapp put it, "The drink stunts you, prevents you from walking through the kinds of fearful life experiences that bring you from point A to point B on the maturity scale."[19] The bud of who we are and might become—our true and unique self—is stunted before it has a chance to fully blossom.

But before we get discouraged and conclude that addiction has singled us out for a life of suffering, it is worth noting two points. First, women without addictions are in no way guaranteed a healthy, pain-free existence—life is full of difficulties, we all have insecurities, we all encounter failure, and growing up is hard for everyone. Period. Second, and more important, as women who have chosen recovery, our lives may unfold in a deeper, more honest and spiritual way than might have been possible without the crucible of addiction. With recovery, we have the potential to transform confusion into wisdom and brokenness into wholeness.

As we begin to heal, it is helpful to understand how addiction stunts and distorts our personal growth and traumatizes our core being.

THE FALSE SELF

"For a long time I was two different people," says Johanie. "I was the person who went to work every day and talked with the other girls in the pet salon and phoned my mother once a week. I liked to look normal. But there was this other me who got drunk every night and broke things and woke up with bruises and couldn't remember anything that happened."

Johanie was living with her boyfriend, who was also an alcoholic, and she knew that the girls at work suspected he hit her. "I let them think that," she says. "That seemed more acceptable than having to explain about the drinking."

In reality, she and her boyfriend were drinking during the week and partying every weekend, at first on powdered cocaine and then on crack. "I told myself everything would be okay if I only did crack on the weekends," she recalls. But weekends started stretching into Mondays and Tuesdays, and her boyfriend lost his job. "We sold our car and I started getting a ride to work with one of the other groomers. I told her my boyfriend had totaled the car. By then I had everyone at work convinced he was this sort of monster."

Johanie started "borrowing" money from co-workers, who felt sorry for her "because they thought I was in this abusive relationship. One of them even let me move in with her after we lost our apartment, but she threw me out after about a week. It was a lot harder to pretend I was this victim when she saw me getting smashed every night."

She stopped going to work and joined her boyfriend in an abandoned apartment building, where they blew his weekly unemployment check on crack in one day, then spent the rest of the week scrounging for alcohol money. "After a while, he didn't want to share the crack with me and I ended up getting into detox and a halfway house," Johanie says. "The hardest part about that for me was I had to get honest. I couldn't pretend to be someone I wasn't anymore. It had been a long time since I'd told the truth about anything."

As Johanie came to understand, addiction and dishonesty go hand in hand. Dishonesty is the all-important, indispensable grease that keeps the wheels of addiction turning. It begins when we first hide the evidence of our early experimentation. "My mom would've killed me if she found out I was stealing her booze," said one woman. "I had to keep up this image of being perfect so I could get into college," said another. "My dad wouldn't let me sleep over at my friend's house if he knew we were getting wasted," another woman recalled.

If nothing interrupts our deepening dependence, the lying gets easier. We begin making up stories—"We were playing video games and I lost track of time," or "We were watching a movie and I fell asleep," or "My wallet got stolen, that's why I don't have any money." The little lies become habitual and roll off our tongue more easily than the truth. In fact, it gets harder and harder for us to distinguish between what's true and what's a lie. The important thing—the only thing that really matters—is that we conceal our substance abuse so we can continue using.

As the line between truth and fiction grows hazier, our sense of reality is further distorted by denial, a form of dishonesty character- ized by minimizing and rationalizing. When we're in denial, we tell ourselves that our habit "isn't that bad" or "so-and-so is a lot worse" or "I can stop any time I want." An alcoholic who regularly has black- outs thinks of herself as a social drinker. A prescription drug addict assures herself that she is only taking her medicine. A heroin addict tells herself that her drug of choice isn't as bad as crack or meth.

Denial creates a fractured inner world in which we habitually lie, even to ourselves. An alcoholic who has been abstinent for two days goes to the liquor store "to buy cigarettes" and ends up buying a quart of vodka. A crack addict who has assured her children that she is done for good this time "just happens to drive by" her dealer's house and succumbs to temptation. The meth addict who has been clean for three months decides to look up an old using pal "just to say hi" and immediately relapses.

In these and dozens of other ways, denial blinds us to the seri- ousness of our situation and keeps us on the addiction treadmill. We may know on some deep level that we have a problem. We may come face-to-face with evidence of the destructive path we are on. But denial kicks in to reassure us that everything is all right, further weakening our grip on reality.

To make matters worse, dishonesty and denial damage not only our inner world but also our relationships with others. Gradually but inevitably, our lack of honesty and authenticity creates a chasm between ourselves and the people around us. We can't show our genuine self because our genuine self is interested in only one thing: getting and using substances. We begin to resent spending time with our family and non-using friends because they may ask uncomfortable questions, because we're afraid we'll slip and reveal the depth of our problem, or simply because we'd rather spend our time getting high. We see less and less of the people we were once close to, and when we are with them, our conversation is full of evasions and lies.

As we push family and non-using friends away, a new cast of characters takes their place: liquor store clerks, bartenders, dealers, and other drinkers and users. But in time, we find ourselves increasingly isolated, even in a crowd. Why? Because getting high is an intensely solitary pursuit. No matter where we are—at a wedding or a graduation party, in a barroom or a shooting gallery—our focus is on one thing: getting our next drink, pill, or fix so we can maintain our chemical high.

Our constant scrutiny of our internal sensations—*Have I had enough? Do I need more? Is it starting to wear off?*—diminishes our ability to relate to others. We find it hard to care about what other people think and feel or how our words and actions affect them, because our own emotions are so numbed and distorted. In a very real and damaging sense, our interactions with others begin to turn on whether we see them as obstacles to getting what we want or as tools we can manipulate: "I won't call my mother because she'll make me feel bad about the way I'm living, but I will visit my grandma because she got her Social Security check and she might lend me some money."

When we manipulate people, we are not interested in having an honest interaction with them. We have no intention of establishing any genuine communication. We are motivated simply by the desire to achieve our own objectives.

As active addicts, we learn to manipulate others in countless ways. "Whenever my husband tried to talk to me about my drinking, I'd start to cry so he'd feel sorry for me and back off," said one woman. "I visited a therapist for months, not because I wanted to stop using but because that was the only way I could get my mother off my back," said another. "Whenever my boyfriend confronted me about where my money was going, I'd threaten to leave him," said another. A woman whose father used to smoke pot with her said, "I knew he felt guilty and blamed himself when I got into meth. So whenever I was dope sick I'd tell him it was his fault, and he'd give me money."

Pity, false promises, threats, and blame are all part of the games we play when we manipulate others. They're part of the dishonesty, deception, and denial that we come to accept as normal behavior as our addiction deepens. These behaviors serve our purpose in the short term—to continue using alcohol and other drugs—but they leave us increasingly isolated and dependent on substances as our sole source of comfort.

Even worse, our deceptive behaviors create a gaping chasm between the woman we've become and the woman at our core. The person we were born to be, the girl with her own talents and abilities, her own hopes and dreams—and, yes, her own flaws and pain and vulnerabilities—is silenced and forgotten under the crushing weight of addiction.

Our newly acquired false self—the addicted woman who will lie and deceive and manipulate to get the substances she feels she cannot live without—discards the girl she once was. Instead, her addicted brain drives her to ever more alienating and dishonest behaviors, sometimes pushing her to the outer fringes of society.

SOCIETY'S OUTCASTS

Tiny was a familiar figure on the tough streets of a neighborhood known for drugs and prostitution. Petite and soft-spoken, she divided her time between selling sex and buying and using drugs. The cops knew her on sight, as did many of the johns who regularly trolled the streets looking for prostitutes. Sometimes passers-by hurled insults at her—scumbag, whore, slut—but she became numb to that, just as she became numb to the violence that punctuated her daily life. Men might beat her, rage at her, rape her, and steal from her. It was just part of life.

One day, Tiny got in a car with a man who drove her to a wooded area. She passed out on the way, and when she awoke she was on the ground with a belt around her neck. As the man pulled it tighter, she struggled to escape. He started hitting her in the head with a brick. "I asked him, what are you doing? Why are you doing this?" she recalls. The memory's a blur, but she knows that at some point he threw the brick aside and drove away. Bloodied and limping, Tiny managed to stumble to a gas station. The manager called 911, but no one was ever charged with the crime. Afterward, Tiny says, "I cleaned myself up and went back out there."

Tiny's life hadn't always been so bleak. She had a good mother, but when her stepfather started making sexual advances toward her, she escaped the situation by moving in with a man and having his baby. She was only fifteen, but she loved being a mom. For the next twelve years, she devoted herself to being a homemaker and raising a son and a daughter. Then Tiny's biological father, who had abandoned the family when she was two, came back into her life.

"I always missed my dad," she says. "I was his only daughter, and I always wondered why he would leave me." Unfortunately, her father was addicted to crack, and he introduced Tiny to it. "My only good memories of him are of getting high together," she admits.

For Tiny, it was a quick, hard fall from being a homemaker to being an addict on the streets. She made frequent trips to detox and was in and out of jail, but she always went right back to the drugs. Her mother took over raising the children. It seemed that only her children could pierce the numbness in Tiny's soul. "Sometimes they'd drive by and see me on a corner, and they wouldn't wave or beep the horn or anything. That hurt," she says.

Like many women who turn to prostitution to support their addiction, Tiny had slipped into the life almost without noticing. "It just kind of happened," these women might say, or "I never thought I'd go that route, but I was desperate for drugs and a man gave me a certain look, and I thought, why not?"

Selling sex is a perilous step on the downward spiral of chemical addiction. It provides an immediate solution to the pressing need to obtain drugs, but it takes a terrible toll on our emotional health.

Like Tiny, women in prostitution confront extraordinary levels of violence, harassment, and dehumanization every day. They have high rates of PTSD as well as depression, anxiety disorders, and frequent thoughts of suicide. One counselor who works extensively with women in prostitution said, "Many of them have a profound sense of loss. They've lost their friends, family, credibility, and self-respect. They're also deeply lonely. They don't like other women because they see them as competition. Instead, for companionship they come to rely on the very men who exploit them."

By its very nature, prostitution is an assault on our sense of self. It requires us to numb our feelings, to offer ourselves as a commodity, not as a human being. It requires us to reject our emotions and deaden the pain of being treated like a disposable object. In a dark cycle of mutual reinforcement, prostitution creates pain, for which we turn to substances, for which we turn to prostitution, and on it goes.

THE TRAUMA OF INCARCERATION

For many women with addictions, the criminal justice system inflicts yet another assault on our sense of self.

Between 1977 and 2004, the number of women serving sentences of more than one year in the United States grew more than sevenfold, according to a 2006 report from the Women's Prison Association's Institute on Women & Criminal Justice. The report states that "Typically, they are poor women of color who were arrested for drug-related crimes. Most have substance-abuse histories, and are survivors of family violence and sexual abuse as well."[20]

One of those women was Pebbles. After struggling with addiction and abusive boyfriends for years, she experienced firsthand the traumatic impact of incarceration.

Pebbles was brought up in the church by a strict but loving

mother who taught her the value of honesty and hard work. "We moved to the suburbs when I was twelve because my mother wanted to get me away from the bad influences of the city," she says with a laugh. "The first day I walked into that suburban school, a bunch of girls asked me if I wanted to smoke some weed. I'd never even seen it in the city."

Wanting to fit in, Pebbles agreed to try it. "All it did was make me choke," she recalls. But something about the experience kept her going back for more. By the time she was in her midteens she had moved on to pills and was selling drugs "for lunch money and clothes." Her activities didn't prevent her from staying in school or from getting jobs. As a young woman, she supported herself by working in offices and nursing homes. She kept her drug use under control—until someone introduced her to heroin.

"A woman I worked with asked why I was wasting time with pills when I could be snorting heroin," she recalls. "I was like, you can snort it? I didn't know. I wouldn't ever put a needle in my veins. That's just not me. But snorting it was something else. Once I tried it, oh, man!"

She became addicted almost immediately, and for the first time in her life couldn't hold down a job. She and a boyfriend started breaking into stores to support their habits. "At first, it was kind of exciting," she admits. "We'd check out the place and figure out how we were going to do it. Sometimes we'd get in through a wall or the ceiling. We'd get this huge adrenalin rush." Sometimes—when her boyfriend was in jail, for instance—she'd break in by herself.

She also started picking up "dates," a steady clientele of men who paid her for sex. Inevitably, she was arrested and sent to jail. Her life fell into a destructive pattern of using drugs, committing crimes, and going to jail, each time with a longer sentence.

In prison, she experienced the harsh conditions that all prisoners deal with daily. She learned that inmates are stripped of their freedom, privacy, and individuality. They are subjected to the use of force and restraint, humiliating searches, arbitrary harassment, and crowded and dehumanizing living conditions. They face threats from guards and other inmates. For minor infractions they can end up in isolation units, which can produce psychosis in people isolated for too long. Pebbles once spent nearly thirty days in isolation for challenging an inmate who was threatening her. "You have to stand up for yourself," she explains.

She survived, but her already-damaged sense of self was further devastated by incarceration. The same is true for many of the 110,000 women living in state and federal prisons at any given time—mostly for drug-related offenses.

Prisons are intended to punish lawbreakers, deter future criminal activity, and rehabilitate those who have been found guilty of crimes. But for women in particular, incarceration exacts a heavy toll and can make existing emotional problems even worse.

According to a 2008 United Nations report on Women and Imprisonment, 85 percent of women prisoners in the United States have been physically or sexually abused at some point during their lives. Many have survived domestic violence. About 74 percent of women behind bars have mental health problems, and 80 percent are mothers. Of these, three quarters have children under the age of 18. The report goes on:

> Imprisonment generates new mental health problems or
> exacerbates existing ones. In most communities women
> are carers, sometimes the sole carers, of their families
> and the sudden change of their role from caregiver to
> "criminal" and isolation from loved ones usually have
> an intensely adverse effect on their mental well-being.
> Children outside prison are a cause of great distress to
> their mothers, who worry about the separation, whether
> the child will be taken away from them or not and how
> they are being cared for.[21]

For many women led there by addiction, incarceration is yet another traumatic episode layered upon the unhealed childhood trauma, the trauma of abusive relationships, the trauma of being used as a sex object, the trauma of losing family and friends and self-respect. And the trauma of a life that has spun out of control.

But our sisters who have been imprisoned are not alone in their trauma. In a very real sense, all of us who have lived through addiction have been traumatized by it, for addiction renders us over-whelmed, frightened, and helpless in the face of our own uncontrol-lable needs.

THE LOST SELF

When we are in the throes of addiction, it's hard to have any sense of who we really are. There's the supposedly normal person we present to the world: a false persona made of lies and pretense, a construct of what we imagine the world wants us to be. There's the desperately addicted person we do our best to conceal: a self-absorbed, unstable creature of shifting moods, relentlessly driven by the rise and fall of the chemical tide in her system. And there's the critical self, glimpsed in brief moments of clarity: a self who is frightened and insecure and lonely and hurt and angry, a self who passes harsh judgment on the false and dependent woman she has become and retreats into the comforting oblivion of her addiction.

In this confusing world of shifting identities, we lose touch with the person at our core. Instead, we define ourselves around our addiction. We break ties with family and friends because we are ashamed of what they will see in us. We let go of hopes and dreams because we believe nothing good can ever happen for us. We learn to see ourselves as outsiders, as people who don't belong in the normal world and who can never fit in. We carry the weight of the children we have abandoned, the loved ones we have hurt, the moral bound-aries we have crossed.

And most frightening of all, beneath the pain and loss and

loneliness and regret and shame that inevitably come with addiction, there is the fear that we have no "self" at all. That we are at our core a bottomless well of emptiness. Even when we've stopped using and are working a Twelve Step or other program of recovery, the emotional wounds can still linger. And without the comfort of our chemicals, the emptiness can seem intolerable.

Ironically, it is there at our core—where we are free of distractions, our false selves fall away, and we come face-to-face with the terrifying emptiness—it is there in the stillness of our soul that we have the opportunity to discover who we really are. For our true and enduring self has never gone away. It has always been there, a tiny bud deep within us, waiting for the nurturing light of recovery to allow it to blossom and bloom.

We will explore the process of healing in chapter 5, but first we will consider yet another assault on our sense of self, one that often goes hand-in-hand with addiction: harmful and destructive relationships.

Journal Activities

Note: *These activities may bring up painful feelings that are best explored with support from a therapist, sponsor, or trusted friend.*

1. Describe the first time you experimented with mood-altering substances. How old were you? Where were you? Who else was there? What was the substance?

   - What was your main reason for trying this substance?
   - What were you feeling before you tried it? Fear? Excitement? Pressure to fit in?
   - What was that first experience like? Positive? Negative? Neutral? What effects did you feel?
   - What were the immediate consequences of this first experience? Did you get in trouble at home or at school? Did you start thinking about using it again?

2. Describe yourself as a girl on the brink of young woman-hood. Were you shy? Self-confident? Angry? Withdrawn? Outgoing? Passive? Argumentative? Curious? Happy? Sad? List at least five personality traits that describe the young you.

   - What were your personal dreams as a young girl? What kind of future did you imagine for yourself? Did you picture yourself as a mother? A wife? A woman with a career? What kind of career?

- What kinds of things did you enjoy doing?
  Dancing? Singing? Playing sports? Playing a
  musical instrument? Studying? Taking care
  of animals or children? List at least three
  activities that you enjoyed.

3. Try to remember when your early experimentation with
   substances turned into addiction. When did it happen?
   When were you first aware that you had become addicted?
   How did that knowledge make you feel?

4. Addiction takes away our true self and replaces it with a
   false self. How did addiction change you? What kind of
   person did you become?

   - Name two or three things you did during
     addiction that you now regret.
   - Do you think you could have done things
     differently at that time? Why or why not?

5. It's easy to beat ourselves up about past mistakes. But
   it's important to acknowledge our good qualities. Think
   about your true, authentic self. Are you strong? Brave?
   Hardworking? Compassionate? Intelligent? Talented?
   Loyal? Funny? Generous? Feisty? Resilient? Kind? List at
   least five good qualities that describe the authentic you.

4

INTIMACY AND THE DAMAGED SELF

∽≫∽

*Have you ever been hurt and the place
tries to heal a bit, and you just pull the
scar off of it over and over again?*

—ROSA PARKS,
civil rights activist

"**I**f it didn't hurt, it wasn't love," Carol says of her past relationships with men. "I was just always attracted to guys who hurt me. It was like the more painful a relationship was, the more obsessed with it I became."

We're sitting at a table in her yoga studio after her evening classes have ended. She pours each of us a cup of jasmine-scented tea. Now in her midforties, Carol projects an image of health and serenity. But much of her youth was consumed by alcoholism and bulimia—and the search for the perfect relationship.

"My high school boyfriend was this macho football player," she recalls. "He was incredibly good-looking and everyone thought we were the perfect couple, because, you know, I was a perfectionist. Class officer. Good student. Pretty and skinny." She sips her tea. "What they didn't see was that I was throwing up every day and getting trashed every weekend. He drank more than I did, and he was a mean drunk. He was always calling me a slut and a whore. He accused me of sleeping with everyone on the team. One time we were swimming at the lake, and he held me underwater until I was choking. Another time we were driving home from this party and he stopped the car and pushed me out and made me walk the rest of the way, because he thought I'd been flirting with some guy. It was almost two miles to my house, but I didn't get mad at him. I thought the more jealous he was, the more he loved me."

In college, she had a couple of serious relationships, both with young men with drinking problems and violent streaks. "It wasn't life-threatening stuff. More like squeezing your arm too tight or pushing you up against the wall and threatening you. Part of me thought I deserved it, that I had done something wrong."

She carried those feelings into her first and second marriages. "My first husband broke my jaw six weeks after we were married," she continues. "I still don't remember how it happened, because I was drunk. I was getting drunk a lot by then, even though I was trying to be the perfect suburban wife. I didn't blame him for hitting me. He said I disgusted him. Hell. I disgusted myself."

When he filed for divorce after three years of marriage, Carol says, "I got down on my knees and begged him to stay. I literally hung onto his legs, crying hysterically. It felt like the world was falling out from under me."

She remarried within a year of the divorce, "this time to someone who was the complete opposite of my ex. Very reserved, very polite. Beautiful manners. I had cut down on my drinking and I had a decent job. So I really thought this was it. This was what I'd been looking for. Except he wasn't very nice to me. He'd make little digs about my looks, tell me I was showing my age, that I was getting flabby, that I didn't know how to dress. He'd point to a woman on the street or in a restaurant and tell me I should try to look more like her."

When he started working late, Carol became suspicious and discovered that he was having an affair. "I blamed myself, of course," she says. "I knew it was because I wasn't pretty enough. I couldn't stand the thought of being alone. So I told him I'd look the other way while he continued to see her." She shakes her head, as if amazed by her own actions. "Can you imagine? Anyway, the marriage didn't last and since then . . ." Her voice trails off as she looks away. "I'm still figuring it out. Why every guy I was attracted to treated me like crap."

Carol was expressing questions that many of us struggle with for years. We long for a committed, loving relationship that will make us feel safe and secure. We dream of a nurturing partner to share life's ups and downs. Yet time and again we are drawn to people who take advantage of us, disappoint us, demean us, or abuse us physically or emotionally. Or we sabotage relationships that seem to be going too well.

To understand what's going on, we should keep in mind that relationships are hard for lots of people. The countless books offering relationship advice, the proliferation of dating services, and the high divorce rate are all evidence of that. But for those of us with a history of addictions, our traumatic past presents real obstacles to forming healthy intimate relationships. What's more, each unhealthy relationship further damages our already battered sense of self. We can come to believe that we don't deserve better and that we are somehow destined for unhappiness.

The trouble begins when we try to construct new relationships on the damaged framework of our painful past and distorted perceptions.

Back to the Future

Renowned anthropologist Margaret Mead once wrote, "One of the oldest human needs is having someone to wonder where you are when you don't come home at night." It is in our nature, she said, to want a close, special connection with another human being. The desire for intimacy is almost universal among us humans. Scientists theorize that this longing is related to the survival of the species: our earliest ancestors would not have survived unless they worked together, and to this day human infants cannot survive without a connection to at least one caring adult.

On an emotional level, healthy intimate relationships fulfill our innate desire to love and be loved, to feel safe and cared for. But unfortunately, not all intimate relationships are healthy. In fact, for women with a history of addictions, our intimate relationships are often a re-enactment of past traumas and a manifestation of our deepest feelings of low self-worth.

In her groundbreaking book *Women Who Love Too Much,* therapist Robin Norwood explained, "It is not so much that the mate we choose is just like Mom or Dad, but that with this partner we are able to feel the same feelings and face the same challenges that we encountered growing up."[22]

In other words, if we grew up with chaos, rejection, neglect, abandonment, or physical, sexual, or emotional abuse, we are likely to be attracted to the same in our future relationships. This is because we are drawn to what feels familiar and because similar relationships give us an opportunity to "fix" situations over which we had no control as children. A cold and critical partner, for example, may give us a chance to earn the approval we craved but never received from a cold and rejecting parent.

But for women in recovery from addictions, our subconscious drive to work out old problems through current relationships is further complicated by the painful legacy of trauma and shame.

The root of the word *intimate* means "to reveal or make known." Intimate relationships, then, are those very close relationships in which we confide our secret thoughts and feelings to a partner who does the same. It is the sharing of the normally hidden parts of ourselves that leads to and sustains intimacy.

Healthy intimacy develops from a place of self-knowledge, emotional and interpersonal awareness, and a fundamental sense of self-worth. But addiction prevents us from knowing our innermost self, estranges us from our own emotions, diminishes our awareness of others' feelings, and damages our self-worth. Even in recovery, most of us continue to struggle with these deficits for a long time. Some women in recovery say that they continued to "think alcoholically" or with an "addict's mind" long after they put down their last drink or drug. Building emotional health takes time, and addiction delays the maturation and healing process.

Until emotional healing is well underway, we carry into our intimate relationships the distorted thinking, unhealthy behaviors, and damaged self-image that characterized our using years—and most likely preceded them.

As we know, our self-image is shaped by a number of things: key relationships with family and peers, the accumulation of experiences both good and bad, and our own genetically inherited character traits that affect how we interpret and respond to life events. And as we've seen, trauma badly damages our sense of self—and *all* women with addictions have experienced trauma. As therapist Stephanie Brown wrote in *A Place Called Self*, "The experience of being out of control is itself a trauma. Addiction is trauma. In addition, many, perhaps most, women in recovery have also been victimized at the hands of another."[23]

Trauma is linked to depression, anxiety disorders, and shame—all of which contribute to feelings of low self-worth. "I hated myself." "I wanted to disappear." "I wanted to die." That's how many women with addictions describe how they felt about themselves during their using years. Those feelings don't just go away when we decide to get sober. They remain just beneath the surface, where we continue to tell ourselves, "I'm a bad person." "If you knew the real me, you wouldn't like me." "I'm not lovable."

Those harsh messages make it hard for us to believe that we deserve a healthy, intimate relationship and almost impossible for us to behave in ways that make healthy intimacy possible. Instead, trauma leaves us feeling disconnected, "different," and unworthy, and severely limits our capacity for trust—the foundation of all healthy relationships.

The beliefs and behaviors acquired during active addiction further undermine our ability to form healthy relationships. Dishonesty, manipulation, and self-centeredness are necessary behaviors to sustain addiction, and we became experts at using deception to get what we want. But deception, which fuels and facilitates addiction, destroys the foundation of healthy relationships. The skills we developed to keep the world at bay as active substance abusers are the same "skills" that make it hard for us to connect with others once we're in recovery.

We're left with a tangle of problems: unhealed trauma, low self-worth, and acquired behaviors designed to deflect—not to connect. And this tangle gets in the way of healthy intimacy. We crave love and support, but we don't believe we are worthy. We desire closeness, but we find it difficult to open up and trust. We want the joy of genuine connection, but we fear loss and abandonment.

As a result of our confusing and contradictory feelings, many of us tend to find ourselves in relationships that are characterized by one or more of the following scenarios:

- We try to become exactly what our partner wants us to be. The way we dress, what we say and do, and what we like or dislike are all determined by our partner's expectations. We give endlessly, ignoring our own needs and desires in our efforts to sustain the relationship.

- We become obsessed with controlling our partner and shaping him or her into the person of our dreams. We may choose someone we see as less capable than we are, secretly believing that if we have the upper hand, our partner will never leave us.

- We keep our partner at an emotional distance. We may be unfaithful or manipulative or lie about significant aspects of ourselves. We won't let ourselves be real and vulnerable because we won't risk getting hurt.

- We accept emotional and physical abuse as the price of having a relationship.

These unhealthy ways of relating are the almost inevitable consequences of unresolved pain from the past. We re-create that pain in a subconscious attempt to heal it or because we have come to believe we deserve it. Or because—filling the vacuum inside us—pain has come to define us. When we carry unresolved pain from the past into the present, we experience it over and over again, endlessly inflicting new damage on ourselves through our past-driven behaviors.

Let's take a closer look at how past-driven relationships work.

"Tell Me Who I Am"

After a chaotic childhood and adolescence that included sexual abuse and abandonment, Grace married a Muslim man when she was eighteen. She drank and smoked pot a little before they got married, but she stopped, she recalls. "He didn't drink or anything, and I wanted to be like him. He was very family-oriented and I liked that. I liked being a Muslim wife. When I went out of the house, I didn't expose any extremities. In our [mainstream American] culture, women expose things that make me uncomfortable. We're an extremely sexual culture."

Grace says that she felt a lot of respect for Muslim women, "although they're supposed to be subservient, which is totally not who I am." In fact, Grace didn't know who she was back then. "I didn't have any sense of myself," she says. "So it was easy for me to say, okay, I'll become a Muslim. I can be this."

It seemed to Grace that for the first time in her life, she had a clear identity. "There had always been this emptiness inside, like there was nothing there," she explains. "When I got married, it seemed to fill that space."

Grace's feeling of emptiness—which is essentially a lack of self—is a common consequence of childhood trauma. Whether the trauma comes from emotional, physical, or sexual abuse, or from physical or emotional abandonment, children get the message that they have no value and that their feelings don't matter. Worse, they internalize the negative messages and reject themselves as being unworthy of love.

When we reject our core being, what is left but emptiness?

In her book *Drinking: A Love Story*, the late Carolyn Knapp describes that emptiness as a hunger that most alcoholics experience "long before they pick up the first drink . . . You hear echoes of it all the time in AA meetings, that sense that there's a well of emptiness inside and that the trick in sobriety is to find new ways to fill it, spiritual ways instead of physical ones."[24]

Like Grace, Knapp tried to fill it by entering into a relationship with a man who could give her an identity, who could tell her who she was. Her live-in boyfriend told her what to wear, how to do her hair, what to cook and eat, and how to behave in public—all under the guise of helping her to become a better person. The not-so-subtle message, of course, was that she wasn't good enough as she was, something she believed in her heart to be true.

The rejection of self and the resulting emptiness inside can set us up for relationships in which we rely on our partner to define us. We then operate on the belief that if we can change ourselves into the person our partner wants us to be, we will find the love and security we so desperately crave. In our attempts to please, we not only try to look and behave in ways that will earn approval, we also end up doing most of the giving in the relationship. That's what Marcela came to realize.

"About six months after I got sober, I met a guy at a meeting," she recalls. "Everyone always says you should wait a year before getting involved, but I thought it was different for Eric and me. We had this instant connection, like in the movies, you know?"

After two dates, he invited Marcela to move in with him. She was ready to move out of the recovery house anyway, so the timing seemed perfect. But, she recalls, "his apartment was disgusting. He was the type of person who left his dirty clothes everywhere. If he spilled coffee he didn't clean it up. There were dirty dishes all over the place. The sheets smelled like they hadn't been washed in months."

Marcela set to work to clean things up. "I figured he needed a woman. No, I figured he needed me to take care of him. I worked for two days straight to make everything nice and clean," she says. "He seemed really grateful, and that made me feel good." But Eric's sloppy habits continued, and Marcela easily fell into the habit of cleaning up after him. "I was doing all the cleaning and scrubbing, the washing, the ironing. I kind of saw that as the woman's role, anyway," she admits. "So I saw myself as a homemaker, which was fine. It was better than being an alcoholic."

But Eric wasn't working, and his unemployment checks didn't cover the bills. So Marcela felt compelled to work all the overtime she could get.

Within months of her move, Marcela's life consisted of working fifty or more hours a week in a hospital kitchen, then cleaning up after Eric when she was home. "I think a little part of me started to resent it, to feel like there was something wrong," she says. "But if I ever said anything, he'd just point to the door and I'd get scared that he was going to dump me. So I tried even harder to make him happy and not complain." She frowns, remembering those days. "It was like I wouldn't be anything without him. Like I'd be nothing. That's a scary feeling."

Like Grace, Marcela's lack of self-knowledge and low self-worth made it easy for her to be with a man who could give her an identity. In fact, her primary sense of self came to revolve around Eric—she was Eric's girlfriend, Eric's provider, Eric's helper, Eric's rescuer. Without him, Marcela had no idea who she was.

But her attraction to Eric went deeper than that. Beneath her endless efforts to please him was the persistent message that she wasn't good enough just as she was—that she had to *earn* the right to be loved.

Eric reinforced Marcela's deep feelings of inadequacy, the past pain that she carried into the present. On a conscious level, she saw the relationship as the fulfillment of her longing for love and security. But subconsciously, she continually re-experienced the pain of not being worthy. The harder she tried to please him, the worse she felt about herself.

"It took a lot of therapy before I could see what was going on," says Marcela. "I was used to rejection, and I guess I was trying to prove I was good enough to be lovable. We were together three years, and when we broke up I thought I couldn't live without him."

In a way, she couldn't. Like many women who have experienced trauma and addiction, Marcela had lots of work to do before she could let go of the idea that loving someone meant losing herself.

"Be Who I Want You to Be"

While some women are defined by their partner, others try to take the upper hand and become the one in control. This was true for Meg in her ten-year relationship with her husband. "I was always the competent one, the smart one," she says with a wry grimace. "So smart I lost everything because of alcohol and pills—but hey." She shakes her head ironically.

"Anyway, I had a master's degree and I was already an assistant director in the hospital when I met Neil. He was in facilities, you know: heating, air conditioning. Definitely blue-collar. I don't know why, but there was something about him."

Meg describes him as "sweet and kind, with a hint of sadness around the eyes." She asked him out, taking the lead right from the start. "Neil was kind of drifting and I decided he needed someone to take charge of his life. Since I was good at managing things, I took over his checking account. Then I started choosing his clothes, right down to his socks. I did his grocery shopping. Then I made him go on a diet and join a gym."

When she got pregnant, they decided to get married. "I don't think he really proposed. It was just this decision we made together." Meg pauses. "He was probably following my lead. He usually did."

The daughter she'd had when she was seventeen was eight by then. Meg and Neil added two boys to the family, and they all eventually moved to a bigger house in a better neighborhood. Meg was earning more than twice what Neil made, and she let him know she wasn't happy about the situation. She urged him to go back to school, to join the Rotary Club, to network.

"I told myself I wanted to make something of him. Isn't that awful?" She bites her lip. "All the time I was telling him what to do and acting like I had it all under control, I was falling deeper and deeper into alcohol and benzos," says Meg, referring to the stimulant Benzedrine. "The bills weren't getting paid, and the credit cards were a disaster. We lost the house. When it all fell apart, Neil filed for divorce and took the boys. I was shocked because I honestly thought he couldn't live without me. The truth was, I didn't know how to live without him."

Meg had grown up with a verbally abusive mother. Her father left when she was eight, and she rarely saw him after that. But she didn't make the connection between her childhood abandonment and her choice of husband until well after she was clean and sober. "I needed to control him because I had so little control in childhood," she says. "It wasn't fair, but I was working out old issues on him. I was terrified to let go of control."

Her need for control was directly linked to her unstable childhood. When we are raised in chaotic households that don't meet our basic need for security, we can come to believe that unless we take charge, everything will fall apart. We cling to control like a drowning woman clings to a life raft, afraid that if we let go we will perish. As Robin Norwood explains, a child who grows up in a chaotic situation will "inevitably feel panic at the family's loss of control." As a result, she says, "We need to be with people whom we can help, in order to feel safe and in control."[25]

A counselor once put it to me this way: control is the flip side of fear. I became aware that every time I feel the urge to check up on, manage, and control my children's lives, the deeper feeling is one of fear that something bad is about to befall them. The more frightened I feel, the harder I try to control.

The same principle holds true when we try to control our partner, except there's an even deeper layer to the fear—we fear that we are not worthy of love.

When we choose a partner we think we can control, we are implicitly choosing someone to whom we feel superior. In so doing, we are acting on our subconscious belief that we don't deserve a partner who's competent, reliable, and desirable. As one woman put it, "Why would someone who has something to offer want *me*?" If we fear that we are basically unlovable, we may seek a partner we believe is more flawed than we are, someone whose undesirability will keep him or her dependent on us.

A certain friend of mine has been clean and sober for years, but she still tends to choose men she has to support. When she married her current husband, she drained her savings account to fix his car, pay off his credit card debt, and cover the thousands he owed in child support. She continually complains that he "contributes nothing" to the household and "doesn't know how to have a relationship." Yet when I asked why she stays with him, she thought for a moment before responding, "He needs me."

The need to be needed is a powerful drive for those of us who feel unworthy of love. Since we are not lovable just as we are, our value lies in being able to "fix" our partner. If our partner doesn't have a car, can't hold a job, repeatedly messes up, or can't function in some important aspect of his or her life, we can prove our worth by making things better.

My friend, like a lot of women from traumatic backgrounds, is repeatedly drawn to needy men because they give her the illusion of being in control—and because they affirm her secret belief that someone more competent would recognize that she is not worthy of love.

"COME CLOSE, BUT NOT TOO CLOSE"

"I wasn't in love with my boyfriend," Tiny confides. "I just wanted to get out of my mother's house because my stepfather tried to rape me. I don't know what love is. I don't know how to have a healthy relationship because I've never been in one. What's love, really?"

Grace, too, wonders about love. She has had many relationships, all of them troubled in one way or another. "I don't think I've ever really been in love," she says. "Not if love means I'm completely free to be myself, that there's mutual understanding and compassion."

Now she's involved with someone who's going through a divorce. "He's awesome," she says. "But I'm lowering my personal values because he's married. I find myself attracted to men who are emotionally unavailable or physically abusive." She pauses, searching for the right words. "Nothing ever lasts forever. But maybe it's a self-fulfilling prophecy, my relationships with men. I'm aware of my tendency to shut down."

Grace and Tiny are like many women whose traumatic past has left them unable to experience genuine closeness. Closeness requires us to reveal our inner self to others—warts and all. It requires us to trust and to believe that we can depend on someone else. It requires us to open ourselves to the possibility of being hurt.

For many of us, the risk feels too great. Because we were so badly wounded by someone who should have cared for us, we learned that the only person we can rely on is our self. We shut down our emotions and mentally went to a place where we could not be touched, where we could no longer be hurt.

Unfortunately, when we carry this survival strategy into the present, we either isolate ourselves completely or we approach relationships with a grim determination to not get too close.

Lisa, who was sexually abused by neighbors for years, had been abandoned by both of her parents. One day when Lisa was a baby, her mother left her and her two brothers with a babysitter. In a note, she asked the babysitter to call the children's grandmother.

"My grandparents raised us," recalls Lisa. "When our mother came back into our lives, we thought she was a family friend. When I was eight, a girlfriend of our mother's told us we had to stop calling her Marie and start calling her Mom because when she went home she'd feel sad and cry. So we were like, okay. My mother told us what a bad guy our dad was. He was an addict and alcoholic. I was fifteen when I met him. By then I was already drinking and drugging."

Lisa says her grandmother was the only person who has ever loved her unconditionally. During Lisa's late nights out as a teenager, "she slept on the recliner, waiting for me to come home," she recalls.

Other than the woman Lisa eventually married, her grandmother was the only person she ever fully trusted. Those two were "the only people I ever told 98 percent of everything to," Lisa says today. But even with them, she held back a part of herself.

"Three months into my marriage, I cheated on my wife with a long-haired girl I found very attractive," says Lisa. "I was full of secrets and guilt. I felt terrible. I loved my wife, but I couldn't love her the way she wanted me to."

The marriage ended in divorce, although the two remain friendly. Lisa is now in love again and making plans to remarry. But she is aware of her emotional limitations. "Anyone who knows me will tell you I'm a giving person. I'm incredibly loyal. I'll give you the shirt off my back. But I can't feel really close to people," she admits. "There's something I'm holding onto. Fear? I don't know." Lisa is still working to break down the walls she built to protect herself as a little girl, to breach the emotional barrier between herself and the people she loves.

Johanie built walls in response to trauma, too. But her emotional barriers present themselves as an inability to be faithful. She has had a "sugar daddy" for almost ten years, ever since the two met in a bar during the bleakest days of her crack addiction.

"We just hit it off for some reason," she explains with a little flush of embarrassment. "I mean, he's married, so it's not like it's ever going to be more than what it is. But we see each other once a week and he gives me a couple hundred dollars and I . . ." Her voice trails off.

Johanie has had two serious relationships since she got clean and sober two years ago. Both men were in recovery themselves. Both were in love with her and hoping for a long-term commitment. But both relationships ended after about six months.

"It's hard, you know?" Johanie sighs. "Because every Tuesday I have to meet my sugar daddy." She spends three or four hours performing sexual acts on demand and letting him fulfill his sexual fantasies. Since she's good at "going away" in her head, she can separate that part of herself from the part of herself that is repulsed by her actions. She just doesn't think about it.

"Then I go home and I have to lie about where I've been, what I've been doing," she says. "And I'm always terrified they're going to find out, and I feel guilty and ashamed and then I'm this total, unbelievable bitch." She blinks back tears. "I know I should stop. I know all the lies put up huge barriers between me and my boyfriend. But I'm afraid to give it up, because what if the relationship doesn't work out? Then what do I have?"

Johanie feels trapped. Her traumatic childhood demolished her ability to trust, so she has a hard time believing that her relationships will last. Her ongoing involvement with her "sugar daddy" almost guarantees that they won't. "I'm thirty-five," she laments. "If I don't stop doing this, it's going to be too late for me to have a normal life, with marriage and kids and stuff."

She's trying to wrap her mind around the notion that her actions somehow fulfill her deep-seated need to shut people out—even people she loves. By living a secret life, she never allows herself to be completely honest or truly vulnerable. Johanie can't take the risk of getting hurt.

But her secrets doom her relationships to failure, reinforcing her belief that she's not worthy of love. And in her weekly encounters with her sugar daddy, she repeatedly re-experiences the humiliation and shame of her traumatic past.

The Abusive Relationship

"Before I did any therapy or work on myself, my perspective of love was you beat the shit out of me, and then you buy me whatever I want afterward. That's what my father did," says Grace. "Or if I'm mad at you, I don't talk to you for a week. That's what my mother did. Or if I don't like somebody and you're talking to them, then I don't like you anymore—all that unhealthy stuff."

For much of her adult life, Grace was one of the many women who associate intimate relationships with pain. "My youngest son's father was extremely volatile," she recalls. "It was really ugly, especially when he found out I got pregnant. He punched me in the head. I had a black eye for a month. It just wouldn't go away. Even now, when I'm run down or not taking care of myself, when I look in the mirror I can still see it."

Grace is not usually shy about defending herself. She explains, "In a bar, if a guy looked at me in a way I didn't like, I'd say, 'What are you looking at? I'm not a piece of meat.' I mean, I'd start a fight."

But she never fought back with her boyfriend. "I was afraid he would kill me," she says bluntly. "He threatened to kill me and my children. I knew he meant it. So I left them with a friend to keep them safe. Family Services took them. I fought for three years to get them back, but I made the mistake of saying that being in an abusive relationship can be kind of addictive. So they wrote, 'She's addicted to abusive relationships.'"

That, along with her chronic abuse of alcohol and other drugs, resulted in the permanent loss of custody of her older children. She stayed with her youngest son's father for two years, even though, she says, "I wasn't in love with him. I was addicted to him. He validated me. He validated my belief that I was a piece of shit. I was a scumbag mother."

In their last episode, Grace recalls, "He had me in a headlock and hit me in the head with a brick. I bit him in the chest." She had finally had enough. Still recovering from her injuries, Grace moved with her son to a battered women's shelter and began the long climb toward sobriety and a healthier sense of self.

Many women—including those without addictions—find themselves in relationships like Grace's. One day, we meet someone who captures our imagination. Perhaps he is charming, affectionate, strong, and good-looking (or controlling, moody, distant, or needy). She may be clever, bright, thoughtful, and fascinating (or challenging, elusive, difficult, or demanding).

Whatever the attraction, there's that special spark we call chemistry, and before we know it we're caught up in an intimate relationship. At first, we're filled with hopes and dreams for a wonderful life together. But sometimes, our early euphoric fantasies are replaced by a growing sense of disappointment, confusion, anxiety, and dread. For far too many women, intimate relationships degenerate into something resembling a battleground. Verbal assaults, emotional abuse, and physical violence become facts of daily life.

In his book *Why Does He Do That?: Inside the Minds of Angry and Controlling Men,* domestic abuse expert and therapist Lundy Bancroft reported that every year in the United States, more than 2 million women are assaulted by their partners, and more than 1,500 are murdered by them. In addition, he wrote, "The emotional effects of partner violence are a factor in more than one-fourth of female suicide attempts and are a leading cause of substance abuse in adult women."[26]

The website Domestic Violence Statistics offers these facts:

- Every day in the United States, more than three women are murdered by their partner.

- Every nine seconds in the United States, a woman is assaulted or beaten by a partner.
- Domestic violence is the leading cause of injury to women, more than car accidents, muggings, and rapes combined.[27]

Domestic violence cuts across racial, economic, and social divides. It affects both heterosexual and gay couples. Both men and women can be victims of domestic violence—but about 85 percent of victims are women.

As women who have experienced trauma and addiction, and whose self-worth is critically low, we are particularly vulnerable to abusive relationships. Why? Because we've learned to blame ourselves when something goes wrong, because we're used to pretending that things are other than what they are (denial), and because we desperately want love and security although we don't believe we deserve them.

When our partner's abusive nature begins to emerge, we are inclined to dismiss the disturbing behavior as a "bad mood," "insecurity," or "anger issues." We overlook the put-downs, the moody silences, the extreme jealousy, the disrespect, the self-centeredness, the intimidation—all early warning signs of a potentially abusive relationship—and try to explain them away. We blame his unhappy past or our own actions. We tell ourselves that if we help him heal from his inner pain or we stop doing "stupid" things that upset him, the relationship will be all that we hoped.

Even as the anger, abuse, and violence escalate, we still cling to the hope that things will get better. The dissonance between our early hopes and our harsh reality leaves us confused, anxious, and increasingly vulnerable. Sometimes we're not even sure we're being abused. The control and disrespect can be so subtle that we doubt our own perceptions. We tell ourselves not to make a big deal out of nothing, and we fail to see our partner's growing power over us.

In the pursuit of power, the abuser's weapons are not limited to physical assault. Abuse includes mind games, emotional blackmail, and verbal attacks that an abuser regularly uses to intimidate, diminish, subjugate, and control a partner. It also includes sexual dominance that dehumanizes the partner—that turns the partner into "a machine to be used for his sexual use," in Lundy Bancroft's words.

When we are depersonalized and treated as an object, the psychological effects can be devastating. Bancroft wrote, "If you are involved with a sexually exploitative partner, you may find that sex is sometimes, or perhaps always, a nightmare. . . And part of why it feels so degrading is that a woman can sense the fact that in her partner's mind she has ceased to exist as a human being." [28]

Domestic violence in all its forms—whether emotional, physical, or sexual—is the repeated infliction of emotional or physical damage by one person on another. It is not about "anger issues" or "immaturity." It is not about loss of control. And it certainly is not about love. It is about power and one person's need to exert absolute control over the other.

Here is how Taneesha—a teacher and recovering alcoholic—describes the downward spiral of her abusive relationship: "I met Tom five years after my husband was killed in a car accident. He had a decent job and was a talented artist. I felt attracted to him. On our second date he told me how gorgeous I was and how much he loved me. It had been a long time since I'd heard things like that and I was flattered. It was exciting."

A tiny voice in her head said that things were moving too fast, but Tom needed a place to live and she let him move in with her two weeks after they met. "He brought his art supplies, his dirty laundry, and his dog. I did his laundry and tried to overlook the fact that I'd told him I didn't want a pet. That was one of the first times I noticed that what I wanted didn't matter to him," she recalls.

Before long, it seemed that Tom disregarded everything Taneesha said. "If I asked him to put away his clothes that I'd washed and folded, he'd say I was a neat freak. If I complained that he burned the bottom of my pans by leaving the heat too high, he'd say I was anal. If I asked him to contribute to the food bill, he'd say I was just after his money."

She tried to be understanding. "Tom had had a terrible child-hood, foster care and everything. He'd been through a lot of abuse and trauma. So I knew he had a hard time dealing with emotions." One day when she asked him to put his dirty dish in the sink, he threw it at her. Another time, when she asked where he was going, he said it was none of her business and shoved her before storming out the door.

"You'd think with all this I'd just tell him to leave," Taneesha says. "But by then I'd got used to his being there. I didn't want to be alone. And I knew he loved me. After every fight, he'd cry and beg me to forgive him. I did."

As the relationship progressed, Tom grew increasingly posses-sive. "He worked the second shift, and he'd call me five or ten times a night to see what I was doing. He'd accuse me of lying. If I was with a friend he'd get pissed. He hated my friends. He called them a bunch of snobs and phonies. I saw it as insecurity and tried to reas-sure him."

Somewhere along the way, she started drinking again. "I'd been sober fifteen years when we met, and I never had alcohol in my house. But Tom kept beer in the fridge. He said he needed it to calm his nerves. For the first few months I ignored it, but he'd urge me to have a drink with him. Say I was being judgmental, that I thought I was better than him. That I was stuck-up. So one night when I was feeling stressed I had a beer. It didn't do much for me. The next day I went out and bought a bottle of wine and fell down the rabbit hole."

With the addition of alcohol, the already volatile relationship exploded. Taneesha and Tom would both get drunk and have knock-down battles. She tried to stab him with a pen. He pushed her down the stairs. She threw his clothes out the window. He beat her head against the doorframe and fractured her skull. They pressed criminal charges against each other and then dropped them. She took out restraining orders, then removed them.

After every episode, he told her that she was the one with anger issues. She was the one who couldn't have a civil discussion.

When Taneesha attempted suicide, she ended up in a psychiatric facility. "I was there for thirty days and they made me go to counseling and AA after that. They saved my life," she says flatly. "It took that time away for me to see how ugly my life had become and to get a little bit of my self-respect back. I threw him out and took out a restraining order to keep him away."

She looks at the floor. "But you know? Even with everything that happened, I missed him for a long time. It took all my willpower not to ask him to come back."

Much has been written about why women stay with abusive partners: the partner may not always be abusive, and "good" times sustain the hope for better days; the abuser may be pitiful and appeal to the woman's need to be needed; the abuser may provide the only or primary source of income, making separation a financial hardship; the abuser may have convinced the woman that she deserves the abuse she receives; the woman may consider abuse "normal"; the woman may fear that she can't make it on her own; the woman may fear for her life if she tries to leave.

For those of us with a history of addictions, the abusive relationship may also seem to offer a chance to "fix" unhealed trauma and prove to ourselves that we are—finally—worthy of love. Sadly, as long as we remain in the relationship, we continue to relive the fear, pain, and shame of our traumatic past. We literally risk our lives for love.

Sexually Conflicted

"I have a big issue with men. I was always looking to men to make me feel better about myself. Even when I was thirteen

years old, I'd be like, 'If I have sex with them they'll like
me, and I'll feel better about myself, and then they'll like me
more.'"

"All the times I had sex and didn't want to kind of made me
numb. Now, it's easier to just do it and get it over with. It's
more for the other person than for me."

"I have a great relationship with a close friend, but it's not
sexual. I've never had a good relationship that included sex."

These are the voices of women who struggle with sexual intimacy—women who experience their sexuality not as a source of pleasure or emotional closeness, but as a source of stress and emotional discomfort.

As women who have survived trauma and addiction, it is hardly surprising that we are conflicted about sex. In fact, many women—including many who have never experienced trauma or addiction—are conflicted about sex. That's because, as women, we receive so many mixed messages about our sexuality.

On one hand, sexual intimacy is idealized as the ultimate expression of romantic love. But pornography and the commercialization of sex portray women as existing solely to gratify men's crass physical needs. Sexuality is glorified as a primary source of female power. But sexual intimacy can leave us feeling vulnerable, demeaned, and insecure.

For women with a history of addictions, this internal conflict is made more intense by our past experiences with sexuality. Substances numbed our feelings, making sexual intimacy an experience of separateness, not of closeness, of make-believe, not of genuine emotion. Carolyn Knapp described it this way:

The sex, if you remember it, was disconnected and
surreal. Your body did what it was supposed to do...
legs moving apart, legs wrapped around his hips, arms

around his back…mimicking what seemed like the
appropriate behaviors: kissing him, holding on to him,
throwing your head back in pleasure even though you
didn't really feel pleasure, even though you didn't really
feel much at all.[29]

Those of us who experienced sexual intimacy as an emotionless
physical act probably learned to view our sexuality as something to
be used, something we *have* that is not really a part of who we are.
As one young woman recalled, "I was able to get anything from men.
It was so easy. Shake your little butt, bat your eyes, wink your eye a
little bit, put a smile on, and you get what you want. And I learned
that the less clothes you wear, the more sexual you act toward men,
the more you get. And that's how I maintained my addiction."

For most of us, sexual intimacy was anything but intimate when
we were using. The numbing effects of substances protected us from
our own emotions and blurred the distinction between fake and real.
Our body was participating but we were disconnected from it, just
as we were remote from whatever our partner was feeling. It became
habitual to pretend and not to feel.

When we are sober, reality is stripped bare. No longer numbed
by substances, we come face-to-face with the emotional damage of
trauma and addiction. Now we feel their harmful impact on our
intimate relationships.

In recovery, we may discover that we are deeply uncomfortable
with sexual intimacy, that it makes us feel exposed, naked, and vulnerable. We may discover that the emotional barriers we erected in
response to trauma are still in place, still creating distances from our
partner.

One woman in recovery from alcohol and prescription drugs
confided, "I don't enjoy sex. It became too painful to try to teach my
husband what would give me pleasure. I gave up trying to teach him
how to satisfy me a long time ago. I had body issues that gave me

a lot of shame, so that was part of it. When I was fat, his sex drive overcame his repulsion. Now, I take care of him a few times a month and he takes care of the house." For her, sexual intimacy has become a transaction that sustains the marital partnership.

For other women, physical intimacy is a painful reminder of sexual trauma. Many women were subjected to sexual assaults, brutality, and rape during the course of their addiction. Many were humiliated, ridiculed, and degraded. In their desperation to get a drink or a fix, some did things that made them feel dirty and worthless. One woman recalled going to a motel room with three men who all had sex with her and then refused to pay her. She said, "They laughed and called me a crackhead whore" before leaving her bleeding and crying on the bed.

For her, as for many women who have endured sexual abuse or rape, the mere suggestion of physical intimacy can trigger intense fear and shame. They may respond to those feelings by avoiding sex altogether or by shutting down during sexual intimacy. And some women who have been sexually abused become promiscuous.

"I work with this population a great deal. These women tend to be hypersexual because they are constantly putting themselves in situations where they are re-victimized," said Dr. Melissa Hunt of the University of Pennsylvania. "They often begin to dissociate when someone expresses sexual interest, so what they essentially experience is that they're being raped constantly except that they're never actually saying no."[30]

As with other areas of unhealed trauma, sexual trauma can lead us to re-create the original situation in a subconscious attempt to heal it—or to punish ourselves because we believe we are "bad." In so doing, we continue to experience being victimized and further damage our already battered sense of self.

Working through the complex and often traumatic legacy of our past sexual experiences can take a very long time. It is uncomfortable and often painful work, usually best undertaken with a skilled, compassionate therapist. One effective technique to combat self-defeating thinking and behaviors is cognitive-behavioral therapy. With CBT we learn to replace learned, internalized negative messages about ourselves with more realistic affirming messages. The goal is not to become someone we're not or to meet society's expectations of sexual behavior. It is to understand our feelings about our own sexuality and come to terms with it in ways that make us feel safe.

In the process, it's helpful to remember to treat ourselves with love and compassion, to let go of telling ourselves how we "should" be, and to patiently give ourselves permission to take the time we need to heal.

MOVING FORWARD

It's safe to say that for all human beings, our beliefs and expectations about relationships are shaped to a significant degree by our past experiences. If in our youth we were loved and nurtured, chances are that we will expect to be loved and nurtured in our current relationships. If we learned that intimate relationships involve mutual respect, compassion, and affection, we will likely expect the same in our own intimate relationships. Those experiences don't *guarantee* anyone a healthy relationship—but they provide a good foundation.

As survivors of trauma and addiction, the difficulty for us is that our past has not prepared us for healthy intimacy. We learned to expect indifference, rejection, or abuse. We learned that we could not trust or rely on others. When we lost control to our addiction, we learned that we could not even trust ourselves. Worse, we learned to believe that we are fundamentally flawed, shameful, and unworthy of love.

These lessons from our painful past lie deep within us. They become part of our worldview, subconsciously guiding our choice of partner and shaping how we behave and what we expect and accept in our relationships.

It is only through the hard work of recovery that we can begin to unlearn the lessons from our past. As we heal and grow, we slowly replace fear, shame, and self-rejection with self-awareness, self-acceptance, and self-love.

In the next two chapters, we will explore the long process of healing. And we will see how all healthy relationships stem from a healthy relationship with our self.

Journal Activities

Note: These activities may bring up painful feelings that are best explored with support from a therapist, sponsor, or trusted friend.

1. What is the first adult relationship you became aware of as a child? Who were the people? What role did they play in your life? How old were you when you became aware that they were connected to each other?

   - What was their relationship like? Close? Affectionate? Hostile? Volatile?
   - Describe a time when one was good to the other. What happened?
   - Describe a time when one was unkind to the other. What happened?
   - How did observing their relationship make you feel?

2. Describe your first close friendship. Who was your friend? How old were you? Where were you?

   - How did your friend treat you? Give an example.
   - How did you treat your friend? Give an example.
   - What did you and your friend like to do together?
   - How did you feel about yourself when you were with your friend?
   - What happened to the friendship?

3. Describe your first relationship in which you felt that you were part of a couple, even if the relationship didn't

involve sex. Who was this person? What attracted you to
him or her? How old were you?

- How did your partner treat you? Give an example.
- How did you treat your partner? Give an example.
- What did you and your partner like to do together?
- How did you feel about yourself when you were
  with your partner?
- What happened to the relationship?

4. Recall an adult intimate relationship that was important to
   you. Who was this person? How did you meet? What attracted
   you to him or her? How long did the relationship last?

   - Describe any patterns that characterized your
     relationship. Did you try to become what your
     partner wanted you to be? Did you try to control
     your partner? Were you emotionally distant?
     Were you abused by your partner?
   - How did you feel about yourself during this
     relationship? Did you like yourself? Respect
     yourself? Did you feel safe and secure? Did you
     feel anxious? Demeaned? Rejected?
   - How did this relationship resemble the first inti-
     mate relationship you were aware of as a child?

5. Describe your ideal relationship. What kind of person
   would you be with? What would your partner look like?
   What would he or she be good at? What would your
   partner like to do?

   - How would your partner treat you?
   - How would you treat your partner?
   - How would you feel about yourself?

5

HEALING THE DAMAGED SELF: A WORK IN PROGRESS

I can be changed by what happens to me.
I refuse to be reduced by it.

—MAYA ANGELOU,
author and poet

"I truly feel that I'm on a spiritual path, and wherever I'm needed I will be," says Grace.

"I still struggle, but today I can think of myself as a person who is worthy of love and respect. And the people in my life are worthy of love and respect. That's a big change from where I used to be."

Grace works for a nonprofit organization that advocates for public support of addiction treatment programs. She has completed a bachelor's degree and is working on a master's degree in community and social psychology. "I want to help people," she says. "I want to inform policy makers and advocate for people in recovery."

Grace is also working to heal her relationship with her children and has built a small network of supportive friends. But as good as her life is today, she says that healing is "a journey, a lifelong process. It's never finished, because you're always learning new things."

For Grace, the journey has been complicated. She dropped out of school in the eighth grade. When she was eighteen she earned a GED (high school equivalency diploma), got married, and started a family. She hoped that her traumatic past was behind her.

But within a few years, substance abuse led to new traumas: the end of her marriage, multiple arrests, the loss of her children, homelessness, and a succession of abusive boyfriends. She had brief periods of sobriety and long periods of active addiction to alcohol and other drugs. For more than a decade, Grace lurched from crisis to crisis, from grief to grief. She was filled with hopelessness and despair.

"My experience of going into recovery was 'You have to do this, you have to do that.' Just so many demands," she says. "I knew that I didn't want to keep using, but I didn't have anything to replace it with. I knew I didn't want to self-sabotage, but I didn't know what I should do."

Near the end of each period of sobriety, she recalls, "I would stop going to meetings. Stop doing what I was supposed to do. I had my own painting company, and I'd meet customers and contractors in bars. I'd tell myself it was for my job, but I knew what I was doing. I mean, if you don't want religion, don't go to church, right?"

The problem, as she sees it now, was that "I hadn't changed. I had only scratched the surface."

She tried therapy a few times, but she resisted facing her emotions. "It would get to a certain point in my abuse history, and I'd shut down," says Grace. "I was afraid to get into therapy and deal with the issues. I didn't want to deal with the feelings. It would come up in therapy and then I'd run from it. And then I'd get into trouble."

She pauses a moment before continuing. "What I really struggled with was the sexual abuse stuff. I felt guilty. I didn't play a part in it happening, but I played a part in my relationships with men. Also the drug and alcohol abuse and self-sabotage by allowing that trauma to keep me from reaching my potential. I mean, I wasn't responsible for it when it was happening, but I was responsible because I didn't do any work to move past it."

Sometimes, Grace "went into treatment to beat the system," she admits. She'd follow the rules, but when she got out, "I would always mess up. Because I put everything together on the outside, but I hadn't done any work on any of that inner stuff. I mean, you can't dress up a garbage can. The inside was still yucky."

Finally, Grace ended up in an eighteen-month residential program. She gradually became ready to face her demons. "I met a woman who helped me through the Steps," she recalls. "That was very emotional." As she progressed, she and her youngest son moved from a round-the-clock staff-support environment to their own apartment "with some supervision, but not twenty-four-hour," she says. "I went back to school. I knew I had to do something different."

Since then, she says, "There have been some really hard things. My mother died and there was a lot of unfinished business around our relationship. My son and I were homeless and lived in a shelter for a while. And I've had to accept my history. It's hard, but I've come to see that it's also an asset because it makes me more compassionate and stronger."

She thinks before adding, "What I've done consistently is stay with therapy and Step work. Recovery doesn't mean you're always happy or that everything's perfect. It's about what's inside. It's a total psychic change, a total life change."

Grace is right. Recovery is not about achieving continual happiness or personal perfection. And recovery goes far beyond abstinence—although that is where the journey begins. Recovery is the long, arduous, frightening, confusing, messy, freeing, miraculous process of learning to know, accept, and love the person we are.

It's the process of healing our *self.*

Let's begin.

GETTING REAL

"Recovery is not a move from bad to good, but from false to real," observed therapist Stephanie Brown. "This is the transformation."[31]

Stated another way, healing is the process of learning to live our own life as it really is. This can stop us cold before we even begin: as women in recovery from addictions, we have likely had a shaky relationship with reality.

Alcohol and other drugs altered our perception. That's what

we liked about them. If we were shy and socially awkward, a glass of wine took away our discomfort. If we felt like a failure, a hit of cocaine put us on top of the world. If we were anxious and scared, a couple of benzos soothed our nerves. If we were sad and depressed, a painkiller or a heroin fix warmed us with pleasure.

What a quick and easy way to escape a distressing reality! Except, inevitably, the effects wore off. Then we had the same issues to face, along with whatever mess we made while we were high. So we reached for the quick fix and changed our reality again. After a while, when the drugs had taken control of our minds and bodies, it was easy to get confused about what was real and what wasn't—to get confused, even, about who we really were.

When we're addicted, we're like two different people living in two different worlds. There's the person and world we experience when we are sober. And there's the person and world we inhabit when we're high.

"Anyone with an addiction leaves herself," explains Valerie, a recovering alcoholic and therapist who works extensively with women with addictions. "A healthy person will be grounded in her body and a sense of who she is. With addiction, people leave themselves constantly. The way they act, the way they talk, the way they think. Sometimes they're in their body and sometimes they're out of it."

Addiction, she says, involves the habit "of abandoning yourself. I'm home, I'm not home. I'm home, I'm not home. Whether it's shopping or drugging or drinking or sex, it's an escape. And once we escape, the way we look at everything in the world is different. And when we wake up in the morning, we're a different person than we were the night before. We only do all that behavior when we're high. Someone who isn't addicted can stay in her body and use all her senses and know what she's doing. The addict doesn't have to know what she's doing. When someone gets high, she does it to not be there."

Not being there, of course, was the whole point. We wanted to escape the pain and discomfort at our core, escape the problems that seemed overwhelming. Besides, for many of us, a fractured sense of reality is all we'd ever known. We'd lived in different worlds most of our lives.

If our parents had addictions or chronic mood disorders, we got used to dealing with Sober Mommy and High Mommy, with Good Daddy and Bad Daddy. If we were forbidden to talk about certain things, we got good at saying one thing and feeling another. If our home life was troubled, we learned to present a false face in public. If we experienced trauma, we had one life before the trauma and a different life afterward—two lives with different rules and expectations. Two different ways of dealing with the world.

In short, if we grew up in a family system in which appearances were more important than the truth, we learned to deny reality. In the process, we came to distrust our own feelings and perceptions.

Learning to trust our feelings is a key building block of self-knowledge. It is through our emotional response to people, places, situations, and ideas that we gain a sense of who we are, what we believe, and where we fit into the world: I'm a person who doesn't like this but enjoys that, a person who reacts this way to these kinds of situations, a person who values whatever it is that gives meaning to my life.

Trusting our feelings also lets us develop healthy boundaries—the physical, mental, and emotional limits that define what we will and won't accept in our relationships with others.

When we habitually deny our own perceptions and emotions, we have nothing solid on which to build our sense of self. We think we saw it this way, but maybe we didn't. We think we feel one way, but maybe we don't. It's as if we're trying to build our character and personhood on a shifting foundation that could be one thing but could just as easily be another.

Our shaky sense of reality makes it hard for us to tell the difference between who we are and who we pretend to be. It makes it hard to let go of denial and deception and learn to live a single honest life.

What does it mean to live a single honest life? Simply put, it means knowing our own inner truths, living in a way that reflects our personal values, and being guided by what we genuinely believe. All of this requires us to experience our emotions and to spend some time learning to understand them. It requires us to "stay home" mentally, to be willing to sit in our own skin.

This can be a daunting prospect. When problems pile up or emotions become too painful, we want to escape into another reality. We want to pretend that things are not as they are. That's why even women with solid recovery sometimes say things like, "A lot of times I wish I could just drink and forget about everything," or, "Part of me wishes I could use again, that I could embrace it again."

When we choose sobriety, we purposely close off the avenue of chemical escape. But we don't automatically let go of our multiple realities. Our long practice of avoiding, denying, and rejecting our own emotions has left us confused and uncertain about what we truly feel. Without access to our own emotional truths, we continue to pretend and to present ourselves as the person we think the world wants us to be.

Johanie has been working on leading a more honest life. But she can still slip easily into pretense. She explains, "I feel a lot of pressure to be this perfect person. My mother's always saying, 'I just want you to be happy. I just want you to have the wonderful life you deserve.' She thinks she's helping me, but I feel like a failure because I'm not that happy. My life *isn't* wonderful. But I feel like I can't let her see that."

Johanie's solution has been to put on an act. "I remember one time she was having a family cookout and my boyfriend had just dumped me and I really didn't feel like going. But as soon as I said I might skip it, she started panicking. I could tell she thought I had relapsed. So I went and put on this happy face and told her everything was great. She was so relieved. When I got home, I cried and cried." She thinks a moment before adding, "At first, it makes it easier to pretend to be something you're not. But then you just end up feeling so lonely."

When we pretend to be something we're not, we shut down the potential for genuine connection. Our inner, *real* self stays hidden and unreachable.

Getting real doesn't mean that we always say the first thing that pops into our head or that we never consider other people's feelings before we say or do something. Awareness of how our actions affect others is an important part of emotional health. That's why we might be a subdued version of our self in church, a deferential version of our self at work, or an outspoken version of our self at home. Adapting our behavior to suit the occasion is part of socialization, part of the normal give-and-take of human interaction.

The challenge for all human beings is to maintain a clear sense of who we are regardless of the circumstances—to not lose our *self* in the process of engaging with others. This can be very hard when our developing self has been damaged by trauma and addiction. It can sometimes seem as if there is nothing at our core, as if there is no *me* there if we are not playing a role.

Johanie has often felt this sensation, especially when she puts on a false face for her mother or when she denies the existence of her sugar daddy. "My counselor said that when I pretend that parts of my life aren't real, I'm losing part of myself," says Johanie. "Like that part of me doesn't exist."

Her counselor makes an important point. When we deny and reject a piece of our own life experience, a hole opens up where that piece had been. Deny and reject enough pieces, and we end up feeling empty or incomplete.

Johanie's counselor suggested that she try to honor her own existence by being more truthful with her mother. "The last time my mom asked me how things are going, I automatically said, 'Great!'

Then I stopped myself," says Johanie. "I actually told her I was feeling pretty bad. So she started telling me how to fix everything, and then I had to tell her I didn't want to listen to her advice right them. She didn't like hearing that, and everything felt really awkward. But at least I was honest. At least it's a start."

For Johanie, it's more than a start. It's a significant sign of personal growth. The more we can let go of pretense and stay firmly in our single honest reality, the more we can heal from our past and become our unique, authentic self.

An important tool in this challenging work is a set of skills psychologists call emotional literacy.

Building Emotional Literacy

Clinical psychologist Claude Steiner coined the term *emotional literacy* to describe the characteristics of emotional health. In his 1997 book *Achieving Emotional Literacy,* he explained the term as the ability to

> . . . handle emotions in a way that improves your personal power and improves the quality of life for you and—equally importantly—the quality of life for the people around you. Emotional literacy helps your emotions to work for you instead of against you. It improves relationships, creates loving possibilities between people, makes cooperative work possible, and facilitates the feeling of community.

Emotional literacy, in other words, empowers us to know ourselves, to manage our emotions in productive ways, and to make genuine connections with others. At its core, Steiner wrote, "Emotional literacy is love-centered emotional intelligence. Loving (oneself and others) and being loved (by oneself and others) are the essential conditions of emotional literacy."[32]

As promising as this idea sounds, it can also be intimidating. After all, how are we expected to know our true self when we've spent a lifetime running away from it? How can we come to love our self when we've learned to loathe the person we think we are?

In reality, we all have the capacity for personal growth. That is the marvelous gift of being human. We are not statues carved in stone, destined to be whatever circumstance has made of us, forever and ever. We are thinking, feeling beings who have the innate power to decide how we want to spend our lives. We can choose to be shackled by the injuries and injustices of our past, or we can choose to heal and grow beyond them. It's as simple—and as complicated—as that.

Throughout history, we see examples of people who have experienced significant personal growth in one dramatic awakening—a moment of grace that let them see the world and themselves with greater clarity and love. The biblical account of Paul's transformation on the road to Damascus—from persecutor of Christians to Christian apostle—comes to mind. So, too, does the story of John Newton, who wrote the words to the hymn "Amazing Grace." A slave trader and later a clergyman, Newton was transformed by a terrible storm at sea that helped open his eyes to the horrors of slavery.

We, too, may have experienced an episode of awakening, a moment of clarity that put us firmly on the path of personal growth. But more likely, our recovery journey has been less sure-footed, a matter of fits and starts. We may sail confidently toward healing on one day—and regress into our old fearful, negative self the next.

That truth hit home for me a few years ago when I was at a family reunion and spent some time with a cousin I hadn't seen since childhood. I had always envied her prettiness and popularity and stable home life, but I imagined I had grown past those feelings. I hadn't. During our conversation she described the beautiful home she and her doting husband were building, and I snapped, "It must be nice to get everything you want."

I was instantly mortified and tried to apologize, but I could see that she was hurt. She soon drifted away. The next day, I made an appointment with a therapist I have consulted off and on over the years. After describing the scene and trying to articulate what I was feeling at the time, I came to understand that my primary emotion had indeed been envy—not of her house or her husband, but of the fact that she believed she deserved to ask for and get what she wanted in life.

From my earliest childhood, I had learned to repress my needs. I had come to think of myself as "less than" others, as someone who was basically undeserving. Even though I had acquired an education and achieved some professional success, those feelings of unworthiness still haunted me. I envied my cousin because she didn't seem to have those feelings. She actually liked herself.

The incident was a reminder of how persistent our feelings of low self-worth can be. And no matter how much progress we have made, there is always more to learn.

Part of that work is understanding the influence of our past on how we experience the present. Our past is where we learned what to expect from others and ourselves, as well as what is safe, what is normal, and what is acceptable. The woman who has received love and approval for much of her life, for example, may interpret a pat on the back from a co-worker as a sign of encouragement. The woman who has been abused, on the other hand, may respond to it as a threat.

I once heard about a women's group meeting in which one of the participants said upon entering the room, "If anyone touches me, I'm jumping out the window." To make her point, she sat next to the window and refused to utter another word. I don't know the particulars of that woman's background, but it's likely that she had experienced trauma, possibly from physical and sexual abuse. Her instinct for self-preservation had taught her that touch was a threat. She felt safe only within the invisible walls she had built around herself.

Sadly, the same walls that once served to protect her now trapped her in isolation. She was like many of us who have experienced deep pain or trauma and who choose to bury our wounds within a protective shell. We wrap them up tight and do our best to pretend they don't exist. We fear that if we get close to the pain or touch it, it will hurt just as much as it did when the injury was fresh. In a way, this isn't an unreasonable assumption. After all, when we have a flesh wound, often the best course of action is to let it scab over and wait for it to heal.

The problem with this analogy is that deep emotional wounds don't go away on their own. Instead, they tend to fester, infecting our thoughts and emotions with unhealthy impulses that cut new wounds on top of the old. The woman who refused to talk to her group likely walked away telling herself, "You can't trust anyone. Nobody will ever like me. I really am unlikable." Her original unhealed injury produced self-sabotaging messages that prevented her (at the time, anyway) from opening up and accessing the healing power of emotional literacy.

For the route to emotional literacy is language—the ability to give words to our innermost thoughts and feelings. Language is crucial to the healing process because we are literally the authors of our own life story. The messages we repeat in our head day in and day out give rise to our beliefs, choices, and actions.

When we use language to examine and understand our interior world, we see ourselves more clearly. We view our past more realistically. And we can begin to write our life story in new ways.

Many of us believe that circumstances shape our life, and there is no question that experiences and people over whom we have no control have had a profound influence on our development. But as we build our own independent life, we carry our past into the present through the messages we tell ourselves. Many of those messages— "I'm bad," "I'm unlovable," "Nothing good will ever happen for me"—took root when we were children, when our understanding of the world was limited by inexperience and immaturity.

Those same messages shape our choices and actions as adults, rising from deep within us, where memory and meaning are intertwined.

It is human nature to look for meaning in events, to make sense of them. When we were little and bad things happened to us or our family, the meaning we likely gave to those events was, "This is happening because I'm bad. This is my fault." As we grew older and encountered rejection and failure, we told ourselves, "This is happening because I'm not as good as other people. I'm not lovable." And when we succumbed to addiction and lived through all its horrors, our personal explanation was, "This has happened because I'm a horrible person."

This damaging and simplistic interpretation of events—a legacy of our childhood thinking—is likely to persist until we're ready to challenge our assumptions and examine our past more thoughtfully. Language is the tool that empowers us to do that.

When we use language to examine our past, we can remove the old labels that we gave to events. We can reinterpret what happened and understand it in ways that rob it of its power over us. Yet for many of us, the notion of talking about our inner pain can be terrifying.

Tiny recalls, "When they told me I had to get a sponsor, I'm like, 'I'm not telling no other woman my stuff. I'm not going to put that shit out there.' It was hard. It was real hard."

Another woman says, "I'm not a social person. I'm not a happy, cheery person. I don't open up to people. In recovery, I try to open up in meetings because I know that's what I should do in order to stay clean. But I have a hard time."

It's hardly surprising that so many of us have trouble talking about our feelings. After all, we've learned not to trust others. We've built up protective walls to guard against the pain that people can inflict. We also feel a deep sense of shame, and we're afraid that if we open up, people will know how "bad" we really are.

What's more, we have probably already talked about our feelings a lot—when we were high. And all that did was make everything worse.

EMOTIONAL VENTING VS. TALKING ABOUT FEELINGS

Alcohol and other drugs can trigger emotional extremes. I remember getting drunk and ending up in nasty fights with my ex—fights about nothing. My emotions seemed raw and real and intense while we were going at each other. But in the morning, I'd feel drained and ashamed and confused. It would be hard to remember what the fight had been about, what had been so important. I certainly learned nothing from letting my feelings boil over.

Another woman, a recovering heroin addict who lost custody of her children when they were small, told me, "Every year on my son's birthday I'd get hysterical. I'd go crazy and cry and cut my wrists or try to jump out the window." She'd pour out her grief and guilt to anyone who would listen, but it didn't make her feel better. Touching those painful emotions only made her feel worse.

Most of us have had similar experiences. During the years of addiction, we endured the emotional meltdowns, the intensity and rage and self-loathing that seemed to bubble up from a bottomless well within us. We lived through the drama and pain and craziness. And at the end of the day, after all the shouting and tears were done, we were left with nothing but a headache and depression, trashed rooms and unexplained bruises.

How could touching those feelings again possibly help us?

Quite simply, talking about our feelings in a supportive environment—with a compassionate sponsor or trusted therapist—empowers us to understand our past in new ways that can set us free. We couldn't do that when we were using because our mind was a chaotic jumble of thoughts and emotions. Truth and fiction were too blurred. Now, with the gift of sobriety, we can examine our experiences with greater clarity and build a more realistic, self-affirming understanding of who we are.

Of course, it is possible to grow and achieve a decent life in recovery without digging into our deepest feelings. Depending on the severity of our past traumas, we may be able to keep our pain buried and function just fine, for the most part. But in the words of Valerie, the therapist who works extensively with trauma survivors, "Clients who deal more successfully touch it. They talk about it. I think the ones who avoid it and just try to move on, they can maybe do a good job of doing that but they have to keep it suppressed. And that takes energy and caution and skill."

The energy we devote to suppressing the past robs us of the energy to live fully in the present. What's more, as I learned from my experience with my cousin at our family reunion, our suppressed feelings can re-emerge unexpectedly, with embarrassing or even shattering results. Valerie explains, "People will defend forever if they don't own [those feelings]. They always have to be defensive because you can't control other people. Someone can say something that's totally innocent, and there it is. And the other person doesn't even know what's happening. So there's a disconnect or confusing behavior."

When we suppress our past instead of working through it, our unfinished business tends to get tangled up with the present. We subconsciously put ourselves in familiar situations, playing the roles we learned by heart so long ago. By using language to explore our trauma and pain, we can begin to assign new meanings to those experiences and to rewrite the old script with greater insight. We separate the past from the present and redefine our self as an adult who is capable of directing her own life story. Then we have the power to create a new story for our future, one based on a clearer understanding of where we have been and where we intend to go.

Untangling Thoughts and Emotions

Emotional literacy not only enables us to replace our self-defeating internal messages with more constructive ones, it also lets us sort out the complex connection between our thoughts and feelings. That interplay can be very confusing, because our thoughts trigger emotions, and our emotions trigger thoughts.

Say, for example, that we're at work and we remember we have a date that night. The thought might make us feel happy or anxious or something altogether different. But clearly, the emotion results from the thought. Similarly, say we've tripped and fallen in public and we're flooded with embarrassment. From that feeling we may have the thought, "I'm such a klutz. I always do stupid things."

A friend of mine was dating a man who was in recovery from a crack addiction. One night he went out for cigarettes and didn't come back for three days. "I knew he had relapsed," she told me. "I felt sick. And then I started thinking it was my fault, I shouldn't have been such a nag, I should have seen the signs, I shouldn't have let him go out alone."

Her feelings of grief and anxiety triggered thoughts of self-blame, the same response she had learned in childhood. It's a common reaction. We don't get the job we wanted, and our feelings of disappointment turn to thoughts of self-criticism: they didn't hire me because I'm stupid/awkward/ugly/unlikable. We remember shouting at our child the night before and the thought makes us feel ashamed. From the shame other thoughts arise: *I'm a bad mother. I'm a horrible person.* We think our partner has been unfaithful and from that thought come feelings of hurt and anger, and from those feelings come the thoughts: *I'll always be alone. Nobody will ever love me.*

It's a circular process, the interaction of thoughts and feelings, a continuous tape that loops round and round inside our head. With emotional literacy, we have the power to stop the tape and give the messages a closer look. Did we not get the job because someone else was better qualified? What can we do to improve our chances of getting the next job? Did we yell at our child because we're a bad mother, or do we need to learn better ways of handling our stress? If our partner has been unfaithful, is it time to ask if the relationship is worth saving? If it is, how can we work together to improve the relationship? Ultimately, what do I need to do to enhance my own sense of well-being?

As we discussed earlier, learning to trust our emotions is one key to a strong sense of self. Our emotions enable us to learn more about who we are and can provide the impetus for personal growth. After all, wasn't it a mixture of guilt and fear and regret and longing for something better that got us into recovery in the first place?

But we fall into a trap when we let our emotions generate the old negative thoughts without stopping to question them. When we blindly repeat the messages from our past, we keep bumping into the same walls and ending up in the same places.

Our feelings are there to guide us, to give us the opportunity to change what needs to be changed and to learn what we don't yet know. By giving voice to our feelings, we have the chance to shift our internal conversation from self-blame and self-rejection to self-knowledge and self-acceptance.

Often, the process requires us to change the stories we tell ourselves about our past. That's what Johanie has done as she works through her father's abandonment. "My dad left when I was eleven," she says. "Until then, I was always daddy's little girl. His little princess. I loved him so much." She blinks back tears before continuing. "I can't even describe how horrible I felt when he left. It was like I was falling through this black hole. Like I was bleeding inside. Like I couldn't breathe. And I knew it was my fault because if I'd been good enough he wouldn't have gone. He was this wonderful man, and I was just—wrong."

Johanie's pain gave rise to her thoughts—that she was to blame for her father's leaving—and that, in turn, caused her more pain.

She spent years running from those memories and trying to numb her pain with drugs and sex. Finally, with the help of a good therapist, she is learning to look at things differently. "My mom and dad were fighting a lot before he left, so maybe he left because he couldn't stand up to her. Maybe it had nothing to do with me," Johanie says.

"And maybe he wasn't this wonderful man but just a weak and kind of selfish man who could only do what was easy. And it was easier to go than to stay in my life."

This new way of looking at the event doesn't take away the pain of her father's abandonment. That hurt will probably always be a part of her. But learning to reinterpret what happened can help her to shed the pain of self-blame.

From this new understanding, she can begin to look at her present differently, too. When something doesn't work out the way she hoped it would, instead of automatically telling herself "I wasn't good enough," she can consider other possible reasons for the disappointing outcome. She can use her emotions to guide herself toward positive change.

Linda, too, is looking back on her abusive mother with new eyes. "For most of my life I hated myself because my mother always told me I wasn't good enough," she says. "She called me stupid, ugly, fat, and selfish if I didn't do things her way, if I didn't do things perfectly." As much as she rebelled against what her mother told her, "Deep inside, I believed her," says Linda. But her work with her sponsor and her therapist has helped her to see her mother with greater clarity.

"I know now that my mother was a narcissist," says Linda. "She constantly put on airs and fantasized that she was a movie star in her high-heeled slippers and silk negligees. She couldn't love me because she saw me as competition."

Linda's new understanding of her mother doesn't erase the negative messages. "Those negative feelings are in the heart, right below the surface," she says. But when Linda hears them now, she can challenge them with new messages.

"I am aware that to some extent I'm selfish and self-centered," she says. "I have periods of depression and when I'm not feeling well, I isolate. But with all that, I'm also caring and giving. And even though I consider myself a loner, I really enjoy helping people. My emotions are like a pendulum. And I've come to accept that as okay."

Linda has worked hard to know and accept herself, flaws and all. Like most of us, she has found that the support of others is an essential part of that life-changing work.

FINDING THE SUPPORT YOU NEED

When we hear that personal growth usually requires us to get support along the way, our initial reaction is often resistance: "Oh, no," we think. "I don't need anyone to tell me how to run my life. I can do it on my own."

This attitude is completely reasonable when we consider it within the context of our traumatic past. Many of us have learned that we can't trust anyone. We have learned that the only person we can count on is our self. The notion of seeking help from others defies what experience has taught us.

And yet, accepting support from other people is a significant milestone in the recovery journey. (We'll look at healthy dependence in chapter 6.) Twelve Step programs and professional therapists offer a safe place to begin.

One of the strengths of Twelve Step programs is that they offer an instant community. As women with addictions, we learned to see ourselves as different, as social outcasts. The experience of getting high was in itself intensely solitary, an activity that turned us inward even in a crowd. Regardless of how social our initial use of substances may have been, addiction ultimately led us to a lonely place. In Twelve Step meetings, we become part of a community. More important, it's a community that doesn't judge us, because its members have all walked in our shoes.

To get the most from our Twelve Step program, we eventually need to "work the Steps." These time-tested principles provide a systematic approach to self-knowledge and self-acceptance, promoting personal and spiritual growth. The intense self-reflection involved in "Step work" is best done with support from a sponsor—someone with a solid foundation in Twelve Step programs who is willing to listen and to share her own recovery journey. Our sponsor also helps us sort out how our feelings and experiences are related to working a good program and staying alcohol and drug free.

As valuable as Twelve Step programs can be, however, this path to recovery is not the only one. In some cities there are other mutual support programs, such as Women for Sobriety. If we're involved in a religious community, we may have a trusted clergyperson or spiritual counselor to guide us in exploring our feelings. Or, instead, some of us prefer to work with a professional therapist. Many therapists use cognitive-behavioral (CBT) techniques that help us replace negative messages with more accurate and self-affirming ones. Therapists can also evaluate us for depression, a clinical condition common in women with histories of trauma and addiction. Since substance abuse is often a way of self-medicating, depression can become worse when we get sober. We may need medication—one of the many anti-depressants now available—in addition to therapy to find relief from this debilitating medical condition. Whether we work with a sponsor, clergyperson, or professional therapist—and often, a combined approach provides the best results—it's important that we find people we can connect with, people who make us feel safe, valued, and respected.

This means that in a therapeutic relationship, *we* are allowed to set the pace. We are in charge of our own recovery. When we are ready to move forward, our sponsor or counselor is there to support us. If we need to stop or retreat, we are allowed to do so. If certain topics are off-limits, we are not pressured to explore them. If we reveal our hidden shame, we receive compassion and acceptance. If we bring up a difficult problem, we are not told what to do. Instead, we are encouraged to find a solution that's right for us.

Our sponsor's or counselor's job is to help us discover our own strengths and truths in our own time. Since personal growth is a lifelong process, it cannot be rushed. There is no timetable and no "right way" to do things. We may do all the Steps in a hurry and then decide much later to go back and dig deeper into some of them. We may visit a therapist off and on for years before we finally feel safe enough to talk about the deep trauma at our core. We may move forward at a steady pace before bumping against a door that remains firmly shut. We progress only as we are ready.

Yet, even if it seems that our progress is too slow or has stalled out altogether, the seeds of healing continue to grow as we give voice to our feelings in our recovery or therapeutic relationships.

Dealing with Emotional Confusion

One immediate benefit of working with a sponsor or therapist is that we learn how to deal with emotional confusion. As we know, learning to trust our feelings is an important step in building a clear personal identity. This does not mean that our emotions are always consistent. In fact, it is very common to have "mixed feelings" about something, or to feel a certain way one day and feel completely different the next.

For example, a while ago, a friend of mine had a nasty breakup with her boyfriend. When he called her three months later and wanted to get back together, she was thrilled. "I've missed him so much. I know we're meant to be together. I'm going to marry him!" she exclaimed happily.

Two days later, she was expressing doubt. "I don't know if I can trust him. I remember all the times he said he was going to do something and didn't. All the times he lied to me. Do I really want to go back to that?"

Both reactions reflected the complexities of their relationship. My friend was honestly confused about where she wanted the relationship to go. I tried to act as a sounding board, but she turned to her therapist to help her figure out what she liked about her boyfriend, what she would no longer accept, and what she would need to feel good about going forward with the relationship. Her feelings were there to guide her, and by discussing them with a therapist she was able to figure out what her most important needs and priorities were.

Learning to Manage Our Feelings

Another benefit of talking things through with a sponsor or therapist is that we can develop skills to better manage our feelings. We begin to understand that while we can't choose our emotions, we can choose how we respond to them. If our partner leaves us for someone else, for example, we may feel like texting her nasty messages. But we can choose to do something nice for ourselves instead. If we get stopped for a traffic violation we may feel like berating the police officer, but we can choose to comply and not complicate the situation. If the thought of going back to school fills us with fear of failure, we can choose to go back anyway and develop a strategy for handling the workload.

Lisa has worked extensively with a sponsor and therapist to learn how to deal with difficult emotions. She put her skills to good use in a recent upsetting encounter. "I was at a gas station waiting in line to pay at the window, and a man cut in front of me," she recalls. "I said, 'Excuse me. You cut in front of me.' He smirked and said, 'What did I do, fart or something?' I said, 'No, but you cut in front of me.' Then he said, 'Shut up, you fucking dyke or I'll set you on fire.'"

Lisa, who used to get in lots of fights, admits, "What I wanted to do was put his head through the window and set him on fire." Instead, she says, "I used my sense of humor to confuse him. I told him that my husband would be really interested to hear him say that." Although there was no way to avoid the pain and anger she felt in response to his cruel attack, Lisa controlled the situation by not letting her emotions dictate her actions.

Like Lisa, we can all learn how to manage our emotions in ways that work for us instead of against us. We won't be successful 100 percent of the time. We're human, after all. But with the support of a therapeutic relationship, we can get better at choosing when, where, and how to express our feelings.

Creating a New Life Story

A third important benefit of talking with a sponsor or therapist is that, through language, we can begin to create a new story of our life.

As we noted earlier, most women in recovery from addictions carry around the internal message that "I'm bad. I'm no good." We've explored how often this self-condemnation started in childhood as the result of trauma, and how we blamed ourselves for what happened to us. Then, when we did bad things during our addiction, our actions confirmed what we had always believed to be true. Somewhere along the way, the line between what went before and what came after the addiction got blurred. Our simple story became, "There's something wrong with me. Always has been, always will be."

To counteract this destructive message, we may be tempted to simply repeat affirmations: "I am a good person." "I am a loving person." "Good things will happen in my life." And certainly, there is no harm in telling ourselves those things. The trouble is, we're not likely to be convinced. Until we give new meaning to the old pain, affirmations are like papering over a hole in the wall. It looks good, but it won't stand up to stress.

To truly change our negative messages, we need to go back to the source, to examine the place where the pain began and understand it differently. Language allows us to do that, to challenge the stories we tell ourselves and to create a new narrative for our life. Instead of harboring fear and self-blame, we can learn to respect our ability to survive and assign responsibility for our trauma to where it truly belongs.

As Valerie found in her clinical practice, women find it hard to break through the fear of talking about the old pain. But the rewards of doing so are significant. She explains, "A lot of women don't want to touch it because they're afraid of the intensity, afraid that if their anger comes out they won't be able to control it. So any remembrance or discussion of the past is not happening. I tell them we can work to keep them safe and to protect them, and to increase their tolerance to talk about it. Because when they're able to re-experience those feelings and understand them from a different perspective, they'll be able to let them go."

Letting go of the painful feelings doesn't happen automatically. Like the stages of grief, working through traumatic pain is a complicated process. It includes acknowledging what happened, bringing new understanding to the past, mourning what we lost or didn't receive, accepting that pain is part of life, and turning our energy toward the future. Navigating those stages takes time and work and emotional support.

For many of us, much of our life energy has been devoted to running from our inner pain. Like the ostrich that denies reality by sticking its head in the sand, we pretend that what we don't acknowledge can't hurt us. The exact opposite is true. By using our energy to suppress and deny our painful past, we continue to be controlled by it. Our beliefs, choices, and actions continue to follow the same old script.

To change the script, we need to change the words we use. That's what happens as we gradually reveal our self in a therapeutic relationship. We learn to challenge old labels and easy definitions. We find new ways to talk about what happened and use different words to define who we are. We let go of labeling our self as "bad" or "victim" and begin to celebrate our self as "strong" and "a survivor." And the meaning we give to our trauma and pain slowly changes from self-rejection to self-love.

With support from our sponsor or therapist, we have the power to literally rewrite our life story. In time, it can become a story in which the heroine emerges from pain, suffering, and confusion to become a stronger, wiser, more compassionate woman—a story in which the heroine is our self.

The Power of Action

Much of our discussion of healing has focused on our thoughts and emotions. But as we know from our understanding of trauma, the mind and body are closely linked. What affects one affects the other. Mental anguish can lead to serious physical ailments. Physical illness can lead to mental distress.

That's why emotional healing requires us to pay attention to all aspects of our life, taking a holistic approach to our well-being. A crucial part of well-being is the belief that we can accomplish things that are important to us—something psychologists call self-efficacy. People with a high degree of self-efficacy approach challenges with the attitude that they are up to the task. They fully commit themselves to doing what needs to be done, and if the results of their efforts are disappointing, they quickly bounce back.

People with low self-efficacy, on the other hand, don't believe in their own ability to succeed. As a result, they tend to avoid challenges and focus on their personal flaws and negative outcomes. "See? I knew I couldn't do it," they say. Each unmet challenge reinforces their negative self-image. Each disappointment triggers the old message that "I'm not good enough." Inevitably, the expectation of failure becomes a self-fulfilling prophecy.

The good news is that each of us has the potential to build self-efficacy. We do it by taking action. Action is the antidote to learned helplessness and poor self-image. It is the path to reclaiming the power we lost to trauma and addiction and taking control of our own life.

The author J. K. Rowling once said in a television interview that finding what you're good at and doing it to the best of your ability is the path to self-respect. In a similar vein, working toward our own recovery to the best of our ability is the path to healing our self. This involves taking action, even when we don't feel like it. Even when we doubt our ability to succeed.

What kinds of actions are we talking about? The answer varies, depending on our circumstances and emotional and physical health. But in general, helpful actions are those positive things big and small that we do to build self-worth. Maybe we're feeling lonely and unlovable. We could resolve to smile at five people that day. (Research has shown that smiles are "contagious"—when we give one, we almost always get one back.) We could go to an extra peer recovery meeting. We could take a walk and really appreciate the beauty of nature. We could start a gratitude journal to remind ourselves of all we have to be grateful for.

Maybe we're feeling depressed about our low-paying job. We could sign up for a training program to expand our career options and then work our hardest to succeed in the program. We could ask our boss for a raise and clearly explain all the reasons we deserve one. We could look for a better-paying job and get help from a career-help center to improve our chances of getting one.

Maybe we're feeling bad about our body because it doesn't measure up to the so-called feminine ideal. We could join a women's support group and learn how to be more self-accepting. If our weight is a health issue, we could join a weight management program and learn how to improve our diet and exercise habits. We could set our own health goals—such as walking more or eating more fruits and vegetables—and stick with them.

The point is, healing our self requires us not only to build self-knowledge, but also to act. Those of us with low self-worth often find it very hard to take action because we've already pictured a negative outcome. We're defeated before we even start. This is when it can be helpful to fall back on one of my favorite Twelve Step slogans: "Fake it till you make it."

In other words, we can act in our own best interest even if those actions don't yet feel natural. This technique works because, as we saw earlier, emotions trigger thoughts and thoughts trigger emotions. Doing something positive, even when we don't feel like doing it, leads to positive thoughts about our self. We smile at someone and think, "I'm a friendly person." That person smiles back or is friendlier toward us, and we feel more likeable. We sign up for a class and give it our all and think, "I'm doing something to make my life better." We go for a walk instead of watching TV and think, "I'm taking steps to improve my health." Each positive thought triggers a positive feeling.

Over time, actions that once felt unnatural get easier through the power of positive reinforcement. As we get in the habit of doing positive things for our self, we gradually improve our own well-being.

In the classes that I teach at a community college, I sometimes ask students to imagine what their life will be like in five years. I ask them to define their goals and explain how they plan to achieve them. A while ago, one woman wrote that her goal was to be "completely happy and have no financial worries." There was no definition of "complete" happiness and no mention of how she intended to achieve these goals. She dropped the class a few weeks later.

Another woman in another class responded differently to the same assignment. She confided that she had been in recovery from heroin addiction for six years. Her goal was to become a nurse so she could help others and make a better life for herself and her son. She worked hard and did well in her classes, even though she failed one and had to repeat it. Four years later, she received her nursing degree.

Today, she and her fiancé have bought a small house together. She loves her job and her son is thriving. Has she achieved complete happiness? Probably not. Life doesn't work that way. But she tells me that she is proud of what she has accomplished and that she likes the person she is today. "It's hard to believe where I was ten years ago and where I am now," she says. "It feels like a miracle."

In a way, every recovery story is a miracle—a miracle that comes from the hard work of putting one foot in front of the other and doing what needs to be done.

Sometimes it's hard to know what actions will help us move

forward in our recovery. Problems can be overwhelming, and there may be so many sources of stress that we can't cut through the confusion. Nevertheless, there is always something we *can* do. There is always some small step we can take. As the clergyman Edward Everett Hale famously said, "I cannot do everything, but I can do something. And I will not let what I cannot do interfere with what I can do."

Taking positive action—such as going to meetings, getting a sponsor, consulting a therapist, and working through our traumatic past—helps us build self-worth. But to fully heal, we eventually need to look beyond trauma and addiction and take steps toward creating a personally meaningful, satisfying life. To guide us in our efforts, the Substance Abuse and Mental Health Services Administration (SAMHSA) has launched a campaign called the Eight Dimensions of Wellness. The program doesn't tell us what to do. Instead, it highlights areas of human endeavor that lead to well-being:

- *Emotional*—Coping effectively with life and creating satisfying relationships
- *Environmental*—Good health by occupying pleasant, stimulating environments that support well-being
- *Financial*—Satisfaction with current and future financial situations
- *Intellectual*—Recognizing creative abilities and finding ways to expand knowledge and skills
- *Occupational*—Personal satisfaction and enrichment from one's work
- *Physical*—Recognizing the need for physical activity, healthy foods, and sleep
- *Social*—Developing a sense of connection, belonging, and a well-developed support system
- *Spiritual*—Expanding our sense of purpose and meaning in life

The campaign defines wellness as "not the absence of disease, illness or stress, but the presence of purpose in life, active involvement in satisfying work and play, joyful relationships, a healthy body and living environment, and happiness." It goes on to say that wellness "incorporates the mental, emotional, physical, occupational, intellectual, and spiritual aspects of a person's life. Each aspect of wellness can affect overall quality of life, so it is important to consider all aspects of health."

Ultimately, the campaign tells us, we have the power to improve the quality of our life through the actions we take. For our life really is the totality of the choices we make every day. When we choose to take care of our emotional and physical health, take steps to develop our talents and abilities, search for purpose and meaning in life, and work to create satisfying relationships, our life inevitably becomes healthier and more satisfying.[33]

In many ways, life is the process of becoming our best possible self. As long as we are willing to learn and grow, we continually move closer to reaching our full potential. We never reach it, because human perfection is impossible. But the richness of life lies in the journey.

Paradoxically, as we learn to value our self as a unique and worthwhile individual, we more fully appreciate our inherent connection to our fellow beings. In the next chapter, we'll look at ways to create healthy relationships and see how connectedness to others enriches the quality of our life.

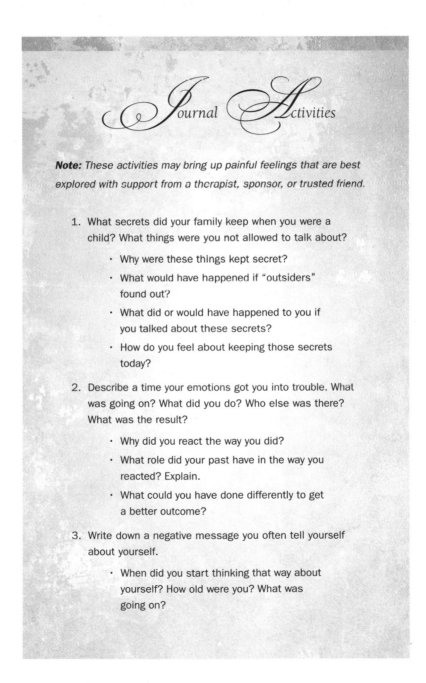

Journal Activities

Note: *These activities may bring up painful feelings that are best explored with support from a therapist, sponsor, or trusted friend.*

1. What secrets did your family keep when you were a child? What things were you not allowed to talk about?
   - Why were these things kept secret?
   - What would have happened if "outsiders" found out?
   - What did or would have happened to you if you talked about these secrets?
   - How do you feel about keeping those secrets today?

2. Describe a time your emotions got you into trouble. What was going on? What did you do? Who else was there? What was the result?
   - Why did you react the way you did?
   - What role did your past have in the way you reacted? Explain.
   - What could you have done differently to get a better outcome?

3. Write down a negative message you often tell yourself about yourself.
   - When did you start thinking that way about yourself? How old were you? What was going on?

- Now think about that experience differently. Write a positive message about yourself, based on the same experience.

4. Describe a time you overcame a significant obstacle to get what you wanted. What was going on? What was the obstacle and what were you trying to accomplish? How did you do it?

  - What does this experience tell you about yourself?

5. What actions can you take this week to work on the Eight Dimensions of Wellness?

6

CREATING HEALTHY RELATIONSHIPS

*Only through our connectedness to others
can we really know and enhance the self. And
only through working on the self can we begin
to enhance our connectedness to others.*

—HARRIET GOLDHOR LERNER,
clinical psychologist

"The first year after I got sober was the loneliest year of my life," says Johanie. "I didn't have any friends. I didn't fit in with people who were using, and I didn't feel like I fit in with the people in AA or NA. I just couldn't buy into the whole Twelve Step thing."

When people in meetings talked about working the Steps and turning things over to their Higher Power, they might as well have been speaking a foreign language, Johanie says. "I could relate to their stories about what they did when they were high, but as soon as they started talking about all this Higher Power stuff, I just zoned out. I couldn't relate." Johanie stopped going to meetings after a couple of months. "I figured I was sober, and there was no other reason to go," she explains.

She was tempted many times to stop in at a bar. "It would have been so easy just to go in and pick up a guy like I used to. At least I wouldn't have to go home to my empty apartment and stare at the walls." But she was afraid to go down that road. She knew that her job, her apartment, and her chance for a better life all depended on staying sober.

"I felt stuck," Johanie recalls. "I thought my life would get better once I got clean, but for a long time it was worse in a lot of ways. I was so lonely."

Johanie was like many women who struggle with a sense of place in early recovery. We no longer belong in our old world of substance abuse, but we're not yet comfortable in our new world of sobriety and drug-free living. We try to avoid situations in which there'll be drinking or drugging. But because alcohol seems to be just about everywhere, and we probably know where to readily find our other drugs of choice, we feel like we have no place to go. We try to act normal—whatever *that* might mean—but we feel naked and vulnerable without the buffer of alcohol or other drugs. It's almost like we've landed on an alien planet and have to learn a whole new set of social skills.

In a way, we do.

The transition from the using world to the sober world is almost always a difficult passage in the recovery journey. During our years of addiction, we missed out on chances to learn and develop the social skills that our non-using peers were exposed to (although plenty of non-users struggle with social skills and relationships, too). We simply didn't get much practice meeting people, making friends, and building healthy relationships.

Complicating the matter, many of us entered addiction with pre-existing feelings of inferiority or social anxiety. Substances masked those feelings and perhaps helped us appear more outgoing and self-confident than we really were. Without our chemical alterations, our emotional issues become glaringly evident. We typically feel awkward and out of place, and we lack the tools to effectively cope with our hidden anxieties.

"I started seeing a counselor because I knew I needed help," Johanie recalls. "I figured at least she was someone to talk to. I was desperate."

Over time, Johanie began to overcome her feelings of being "completely different" from everyone else. She learned that many people—even those whose lives seem carefree—struggle with social anxiety, shyness, and self-consciousness. Like them, Johanie's challenge was to learn how to manage her anxieties so she could connect with others in a genuine way. Working closely with her therapist, Johanie slowly became more comfortable opening up to others.

"I ended up going back to meetings because I wanted to meet people I could relate to, people who understand what I've been through," she says. Even though it's frowned upon to seek romantic relationships in AA and NA meetings, Johanie admitted, "My first thought was that maybe I'd find a boyfriend." She did—in fact, two of them—but both relationships fell apart "because I still had so much work to do on myself," she admits.

Eventually Johanie developed a friendship with a woman who shares her love of animals. "For the first time in years, I have a female friend I can talk to and hang out with. Like two normal people, you know?" she says. "I used to be one of those women who only got along with men. I saw women as competition. Now I'm so grateful that I have a female friend. It's probably the best relationship I've had in a long time."

Johanie continues to struggle with feelings of insecurity and low self-worth, but she also sometimes feels an emotion she's less familiar with—happiness.

"I still have a long way to go, but my life is pretty good right now," she says. "It may not sound like a lot, but actually having a friend who understands me, who's there for me—that's important. And I try to be there for her. We all need someone we can count on."

As Johanie's journey of healing progresses, she has come to recognize that healthy relationships are essential to well-being. We humans are social creatures, and women, especially, depend on satisfying relationships to enhance our sense of comfort and security and to enrich the quality of our life. Our bonds with our intimate partner, family, friends, co-workers, and others help shape our sense of self, and they have a profound impact on our emotional health.

Yet as women who are healing from substance and behavioral addictions, we may believe that we have little control over the quality of our relationships. We may have "learned" that relationships inevitably result in disappointment and pain. We may even have given up on the notion of forming relationships at all, preferring instead to live in self-imposed isolation or keeping our relationships superficial.

In reality, we all have the capacity to create the kinds of relationships that nurture and sustain us. Doing so requires us to let go of destructive beliefs and behaviors and to practice the skills that promote genuine connection.

Let's begin by examining the role of independence, dependence, and codependence in relationships.

RETHINKING INDEPENDENCE, DEPENDENCE, AND CODEPENDENCE

Twelve Step programs succeed so well partly because they are grounded in two enduring truths: first, that personal growth involves a progression from unhealthy dependence to healthy independence, and second, that healthy independence includes the capacity for healthy dependence.

Recovery from substance and behavioral addictions empowers us to undo—or at least address—the damage of our past and develop a more positive sense of self. In the process, we accept responsibility for our choices and actions and begin to gain control over our life. We become responsible, independent adults—not *perfect* adults, because human perfection is impossible, but adults who are capable of acting in our own best interest.

But healthy, independent adults do not exist in a vacuum. We live within a tapestry of people and relationships that are woven into the fabric of our life. The healthy, independent self is, in fact, part of a greater whole.

Much of the work of healing turns us inward, to the memories, thoughts, emotions, and aspirations that have shaped our sense of self. Understanding our past with greater clarity and tapping into our inner strengths are essential elements of the healing process. But healing requires us to look outward as well, to the relationships that influence our personal identity. The people in our life, past and present, have a profound impact on how we see ourselves. Unhealthy relationships hurt and diminish us, while healthy ones nurture our growth and well-being.

Most healthy adult relationships are built on a delicate balance of independence and dependence: *I am an individual with a separate identity, yet I know that I can depend on you when I need to.* There is no deep connection between people without some degree of dependence.

At first, this concept can seem confusing. Many of us are used to thinking of independence as good and dependence as bad. We have no problem with accepting the importance of achieving independence. That's what most of us are striving for, the ability to direct and control the course of our own life. But accepting that we should also be dependent is a lot less appealing. In our experience, dependence is a sign of weakness and neediness, a vulnerable state linked to damaging relationships and destructive behaviors.

As women, we may feel that dependence made us vulnerable to abuse and exploitation. We remember the helplessness we felt when we were traumatized as children, or when an abusive partner hurt us, or when we lost control of our lives to our own addiction. We naturally fear experiencing that helplessness again. In our determination to protect ourselves, we may equate independence with total self-sufficiency and dependence with danger. We think that if we don't depend on anyone, we won't get hurt.

But all healthy relationships contain elements of give and take. We depend on our family and friends to listen to us when we are troubled, to give us a hand when we need help, to boost our morale when we're feeling low, and to share our happiness when things go well. Healthy dependence doesn't mean that we expect others to rescue or take care of us. It means that we can depend on the people we care about to be there for us—and they can depend on us to do the same for them. This mutual dependency is what enables relation-ships to grow.

In a way, when we talk about healthy dependence, we're also talking about personal boundaries. Boundaries are the set of physi-cal and emotional limits we develop to define our self and protect us from manipulation and abuse. They're the internal guidelines that reflect our values and beliefs. They empower us to negotiate what we will and won't accept in relationships. Boundaries enable us to say to others, "This is who I am. This is what I need. I respect your boundaries and I expect you to respect mine."

We're not born with well-defined boundaries the way we're born with a certain hair color or body type. Rather, boundaries develop and evolve as we tune in to our own emotional responses to people and circumstances. By listening to our emotions, we discover what is important to us, what makes us uncomfortable, and what makes us feel safe. Personal boundaries make us strong enough to risk healthy dependence in a relationship because we have a clear sense of what we need, what we value, and what lines we won't allow to be crossed.

As women who have experienced trauma and addiction, we have personal boundaries that have been repeatedly violated. We learned that our need for safety, security, and respect didn't matter. We learned that our emotional health was of no concern to people we trusted and needed to be there for us. We learned that our values and beliefs could be swept aside by people with power over us. Over time, it almost seemed as if we had no boundaries at all, as if others could do whatever they wished to us.

In response to that horrible sense of powerlessness, some of us erected walls to keep others out. We decided that the only way to be safe was to never allow anyone to get close to us, to never depend on anyone. We developed an *unhealthy* independence that limited the possibility of genuine connection with others.

On the other hand, some of us went to the other extreme. With no clear sense of boundaries, we lost our *self* in our relationships. Instead of having all walls and no connection, we had no walls and became completely enmeshed. We became codependent.

In a codependent relationship, there's no "me" without our partner. All of our energies are focused on "fixing" or pleasing or hanging onto the object of our obsession. Our life seems to have value only to the extent that we are connected to him or her. Instead of focusing on our *self* and trying to become the best person we can be, we give all of our love and attention and care to our partner.

The classic example of codependence is the alcoholic's wife who makes it her life's mission to rescue her husband. She watches his every move, chastises him when he slips up, and pressures him to do what she thinks is best. Her own needs and feelings don't matter. She lives only through him.

It was to help such women that Al-Anon was founded, based on the principle that codependence is as potentially damaging as alcoholism itself. Since then, codependence has become widely recognized as an unhealthy relationship pattern that affects not only spouses and families of addicts but anyone whose life is controlled by another's needs—real or perceived.

Valerie, the therapist we met earlier, says that while some women in recovery struggle for years with an inability to trust, others seem to trust instantly, "and that's part of the problem. There are no boundaries. They want to be loved, they want to be protected, so they think if they give their trust immediately and completely they'll get love," she says. "And I tell them no. You can't give it away, like you can't give sex away and think it's going to get something. Trust, dependence— it has to be an honest and interactive thing."

On the website EssentialLifeSkills.net, Zorka Hereford, author of the book *Nine Essential Life Skills,* asserts that our personal boundaries need work if we engage in some of the following behaviors:

- Going against personal values or rights in order to please others

- Letting others define you
- Expecting others to fill your needs automatically
- Feeling bad or guilty when you say no
- Not speaking up when you are treated poorly
- Falling "in love" with someone you barely know or who reaches out to you
- Accepting advances, touching, and sex that you don't want
- Touching a person without asking[34]

I would add to that list the inability to let others get close to us. For boundaries are as much about defining what we need as defining what we don't want: *I need this from you in order to feel good about our relationship*. And for all our fear of getting hurt, having people in our life we can trust and depend on is a basic human need. When we deny that need, we deprive ourselves of an essential component of emotional health. Healthy dependence helps to heal the pain of our past by assuring us that we are worthy of being cared for, that our needs and feelings do matter.

Healthy dependence doesn't happen automatically in relationships. It develops slowly over time as the people involved reveal more of themselves little by little. Shared experiences and shared emotions gradually create a sense of trust that we can depend on each other for honesty, support, and validation.

In healthy relationships, we are independent enough to maintain our own identity and trusting enough to depend on others. Our boundaries help us define the degree to which we remain separate and the degree to which we come together. Because relationships change as people grow and evolve, the degrees of independence and dependence shift over time. But the essential elements of separate identities and mutual dependence remain.

How do we build both independence and healthy dependence in relationships? One important way is through communication—the ability not only to express our own thoughts and feelings but to listen to and empathize with the thoughts and feelings of others.

The Fine Art of Communication

As we saw in our discussion of emotional literacy, words empower us to examine, understand, and give meaning to our emotions. With emotional literacy, we become increasingly able to make sense of our own inner world. But it also helps us to understand and connect with others. As we gain skill in using the building blocks of effective communication—"I" statements, listening skills, and empathy—we begin to create honesty and trust in our relationships.

"I" Statements

All relationships involve conflict. Our partner doesn't react the way we hoped she would. Our friend disagrees with our point of view. Our sister backs out of her promise to baby-sit our kids. When we're hurt or disappointed, our first instinct may be to use "you" statements: "You're a thoughtless person." "You're holding my past against me." "You don't care about my feelings."

We react this way when we *assume* that we know what motivated someone's actions. Assumptions like these cut the lines of communication before they're even connected. When we assume that we know what someone else is thinking, we're actually tuning in to what's going on inside our *own* head.

We've all had our assumptions proven wrong sometimes. For example, we might assume that a neighbor didn't say hello because she's mad at us, when in fact she didn't even see us. We might assume that our son was irritable during dinner because he couldn't borrow the car, when he was really thinking about his recent spat with his girlfriend. We might assume that a prospective employer hasn't phoned us because we blew the job interview, when in reality she's been called out of town.

A friend of mine has had a strained relationship with her grown daughter. Recently, when her daughter failed to show up for a dinner date, my friend assumed that her daughter was thoughtlessly blowing her off. She left a scathing message on her daughter's phone, saying something like, "You don't care how I feel. You think of no one but yourself." Later on, she was ashamed when she learned that her daughter had been stuck in a massive traffic jam and that she had forgotten her cell phone. Their difficult relationship was further damaged by my friend's assumptions.

We can avoid this type of miscommunication when we learn to express our feelings with "I" statements. Instead of saying, "You don't care about my feelings," we can say something like, "I feel hurt. I want a relationship with you but it seems to me like you only come around when you want me to do something for you. I need you to recognize my feelings more." Instead of saying, "You're selfish," we can say, "I have the sense sometimes that my needs aren't important to you. Is there something I can do to better let you know what I need?" Instead of saying, "You'll never forgive me for my past," we can say, "I get the feeling that you hold some things against me. Can we talk about it?"

When we say, "You feel this," or "You think that," we're on shaky ground. We can never safely assume that we know what someone else is thinking or feeling. But when we say, "I feel this," or "I believe that," we move our conversation away from guesswork and onto solid ground. By stating our thoughts and feelings honestly and directly, we open the door to meaningful communication.

But genuine communication is never one-sided. In addition to expressing ourselves as clearly as possible, we need to listen to what is being said.

Listening

Holistic healer Dr. Rachel Naomi Remen wrote, "The most basic and powerful way to connect to another person is to listen. Just listen." When we say, "Tell me how you feel," or "Help me understand how you see it," we are creating a trusting environment in which our relationships can flourish.

For many of us, communication consists of waiting for the other person to stop talking so we can jump in. Sometimes we don't even wait for the person to finish before we interject our take on the matter.

I was often that way with my ex-husband, and the situation got worse as our marriage deteriorated. One day when we were raking the yard, he started talking about a co-worker who had quit his job and gone back to school. I knew my husband felt stuck in his job, and that worried me. But instead of drawing him out on the subject, I immediately said, "Well, we can't afford for you to quit your job. So don't even think about it."

Was he considering quitting his job at that time? I'll never know. What I do know is that if I'd been willing to listen, we might have had a real conversation about his employment situation, and that could have made us both feel better. Instead, I made the conversation about what I wanted to say and closed the door to a meaningful exchange.

Real listening goes beyond hearing the words that are said. It's listening from the heart to the emotions behind the words. It's the foundation of genuine connection.

Tiny, who has two years of recovery after eleven years on the streets, understands the power of listening. "There are not a lot of people that I trust. If I'm hurting, I'm not going to tell you. I have a smile on my face and keep walking," she says. "But today I have three women I can really tell what's going on in my life. I can just call and they'll listen. Just for that person to listen is a huge thing."

She is also ready to listen when her friends need support from her. By listening from the heart, Tiny and her friends are helping each other to heal and strengthening their relationships through the power of empathy.

Empathy

Empathy is the ability to share another's feelings, to walk in her shoes. Rather than simply observing that our friend or partner is sad, for example, we can imagine the depth of her feelings. We almost experience the feelings with her. The role of empathy is not to subject us to another's suffering, but to deepen our connection to her emotional state and to ease the human burden of loneliness.

Spirituality writer Sharon Salzberg wrote in *Lovingkindness: The Revolutionary Art of Happiness*:

> Throughout our lives we long to love ourselves more
> deeply and to feel connected to others. Instead, we often
> contract, fear intimacy, and suffer a bewildering sense
> of separation. We crave love, and yet we are lonely. Our
> delusion of being separate from one another, of being
> apart from all that is around us, gives rise to all of this
> pain.[35]

With empathy, we begin to understand that we are not as different from everyone else as we may have imagined. We learn that we all have feelings ranging from despair and hopelessness to delight and joy and that our similarities usually outweigh our differences. When we share emotions with others, our sense of connectedness grows and our relationships become more meaningful. We *get* where someone is coming from, and we have the comforting sense that she understands us, as well.

Empathy also sharpens our awareness of how our words and actions affect others. When we were addicted or struggling with the turmoil of trauma, anxiety, depression, and other emotional health issues, our world was intensely self-centered. In our pain, we may have hurt others, unable to imagine how our actions made them feel. My friend Meg admits that during the height of her prescription drug addiction, she routinely lashed out at her husband.

"I was a wreck, but I didn't know it," she says. "I belittled him, humiliated him, called him weak and spineless. I told myself I wanted him to be more manly, but all I did was tear him down. I never once thought about how that made him feel. It was like I was emotionally blind."

She also gave little thought to the impact of her frequent rages on her children. "I look back on myself then, and I'm so ashamed," says Meg. "I never thought about how scared those kids must have been, listening to their mother turn into a crazy woman. It must have been awful, but I didn't see it."

As Meg's capacity for empathy grew over the course of her recovery, she was able to imagine the impact of her behavior on her ex-husband and children. "It was painful," she says. "The shame was awful. It still is, at times. But the only thing I can do is tell them how sorry I am and try to make it up to them. Today, I'm always kind to my ex and as loving to my kids as they'll let me be."

Meg can't take away her children's memories of what she did, but she can help them build new memories of her kindness and love. Empathy—the ability to put herself in their shoes—is the skill she needed to improve her relationship with her children. It empowers her to help heal their pain and to work through her own sense of shame.

Empathy is essential to healthy relationships. It moves us out of the role of observer and into the role of participant. Through our shared emotional experiences, we deepen our connection to others and strengthen the healing bond of our common humanity.

MANAGING OUR EXPECTATIONS

Relationships come with built-in expectations: If we email a friend we'll get a response; if we do someone a favor we'll receive a thank-you; if we invite people to our home they'll show up on time. Dozens of everyday expectations form a kind of social contract that keeps the wheels of social interaction running smoothly.

But problems crop up when people in a relationship have different expectations or when we don't communicate them clearly. The truth of this hit home for me a while back when I began dating a wonderful man. Friends of his, a married couple, invited us to dinner at their home. After visiting for a while, the wife went into the kitchen to finish preparing the meal. I followed her and offered to help, but she assured me that she had everything under control and urged me to make myself comfortable in the living room. Not wanting to get in the way, I rejoined the men.

Later, during the meal, I noticed my companion giving me icy looks. On the drive home he was quiet but claimed that nothing was bothering him. I didn't hear from him until he called a few days later to apologize. "I thought you should have been in the kitchen helping her," he admitted. "That's what my mother would have done, so I thought that's what you should have done."

He was very understanding when I explained that his friend had made it clear she didn't want my help. His unspoken expectations had put a damper on an otherwise enjoyable evening.

Such misunderstandings happen all the time. We expect someone to call while he's out of town, but he expects that we know he'll be too busy. We expect a new romantic partner to hold our hand when we're walking, but she expects that we'll be embarrassed by a public display of affection. We expect our date to pay for the movie, but he expects that we'll split the cost. We all enter relationships with expectations based on past experiences and what we consider "normal."

Nowhere, perhaps, do our expectations play a greater role than in our romantic relationships. As women, many of us were raised on fairytales that assured us of our right to be treated as a princess. Even some otherwise ardent feminists may subconsciously harbor the notion that a romantic partner will put them on a pedestal and endeavor to meet their every need, simply because generations of women have been programmed to expect that. Reconciling those childhood expectations with the adult world of personal responsibilities and shared obligations may require us to carefully examine what we truly value and need in an intimate relationship.

Too often, we expect people to read our mind and intuit our

expectations. In reality, it is up to us to clarify our expectations. This can be hard to do. As women, we are often taught to be passive and agreeable, to put others' needs before our own. When we do speak up, some people might still label us as unfeminine or even bitchy. Despite societal attitudes, we are responsible for clarifying what we want and need in our personal relationships, not in an aggressive way (which conveys disrespect and anger), but in an assertive way that conveys respect and clarity.

"Many women in early recovery tend to be either passive or aggressive," observes Valerie. "You don't really get the results you were looking for with either of those approaches. If you're passive, you don't get valued. You don't get respect. If you're aggressive, you get more of an attitude about your behavior."

The woman who fumes silently while her family goes off to watch television and leaves her with a kitchen full of dirty dishes, or who grits her teeth and says nothing when her son repeatedly brings the car home with the gas tank near empty, has failed to make her expectations clear.

It's true that clarifying expectations does not guarantee that family members will pitch in with the dishes or put gas in the car. But having a discussion about expectations at least opens the door to negotiation and creates an environment where understanding, compromise, and change can happen.

A friend of mine, Bianca, learned the value of clear expectations one Christmas Eve when she hosted her traditional family gathering in her home. The family was reeling from revelations of Bianca's grown son's substance abuse, financial struggles, and marital problems, including an affair with his wife's best friend.

"I made a decision to have everyone over as usual—my kids, grandkids, nephews, his estranged wife—everyone," Bianca said. "But I told everyone as they arrived that I wasn't going to permit one negative thing. The kids deserved a good Christmas and we were going to give it to them. And every time someone started to say

something negative, I said no. There was no pretending that something hadn't happened. It just wasn't the focus that evening. And we
had fun. We played games, laughed. It was beautiful."

She explained, "I had made that decision. I made the rules. And
once that was clear, everyone knew what the rules were and we could
just relax." By setting the rules and explicitly stating her expectations,
she made it easier for her family to enjoy their time together.

THE ROLES WE PLAY

Building healthy relationships requires us not only to strengthen our
communication skills, but also to let go of destructive behavior patterns. These include casting ourselves into self-defeating roles and
getting caught up in something called the "Drama Triangle."

Family Roles

As women in recovery from trauma and addiction, we have undoubtedly been touched by family dysfunction. Some people claim that
most families are dysfunctional in one way or another, and there's an
element of truth in this. After all, we humans are full of contradic-
tions and character flaws, and when we're together in a close unit—
such as a family—conflict and unhealthy dynamics sometimes arise.

But a dysfunctional family is not simply a collection of people
who don't always get along. It is one in which the growth of its
individual members is sacrificed to the perceived internal balance
and security of the family unit. Family members are handicapped in
their emotional development by the roles they assume to preserve the
family system, to keep it from falling apart or changing. Family therapist Sharon Wegscheider-Cruse first identified five common dysfunctional family roles: caretaker, hero, lost child, clown, and scapegoat.

The caretaker is the problem-solver who fixes everything, and in
the process probably does a lot of enabling. The hero is the over-
achiever who strives to be perfect and maintain the family's good
image. The lost child tries to reduce the family's stress by having

no individual needs and causing no problems. The clown acts the playful fool to make the situation seem less dire. And the scape-goat—often the alcoholic or addict—becomes the sole source and repository of the family's problems and unhappiness. The scapegoat is blamed for everything.

Such roles do great damage to our sense of identity. We can become defined by the parts we play, boxed in by prescribed notions of self that limit our vision of who we are or what we can accomplish. We may be accustomed, for example, to being told we're not capable of figuring things out on our own or that we're the cause of everyone else's problems. We may have come to believe that we really are infe-rior to the rest of our family, that we lack ability, talent, brains, good sense, or whatever it is that others have and we supposedly don't. We may have become resigned to being the "loser" in the family.

And in reality, some of these negative perceptions are the result of our past behavior, the inevitable consequences of our past mistakes. But if we take a step back and look at ourselves with compassion and understanding, we begin to see that there is a difference between what we did and who we are—that our true, authentic self does not fit into that narrow role. That narrow view ignores our many talents, strengths, and abilities. We are bigger and better than the limiting role of our past.

Sometimes, family members continue to see us in our old scape-goat role long after we are well into our recovery. As painful as this may be, we have no control over *their* personal growth. It takes time for long-held perceptions to change, and our responsibility is to attend to our own healing. As we let go of our old roles and become more truly our self, we foster our own personal growth, form authen-tic connections, and indirectly improve the family unit.

The Drama Triangle

In the 1960s, Dr. Stephen Karpman introduced a different way of looking at the roles we play. He created a behavioral model called the Drama Triangle, which consists of three roles: persecutor, victim, and rescuer. Interestingly, it requires only two actors. Each person constantly changes roles as the scene unfolds.[36]

To see how it works, consider the following scenario. Shannon discovers that the household checking account is short because her boyfriend, Kevin, bought himself two new video games. She calls him into the kitchen, where she's been paying bills online.

Shannon (persecutor): I can't believe it! You knew we were short of money this month, but you went out and bought yourself video games.

Kevin (victim): Yeah, well, maybe I wouldn't have if you were ever home. What am I supposed to do when you're out five nights a week? Sit here and twiddle my thumbs?

Shannon (victim): You know I have to go to meetings. That's the only way I'm going to stay clean. But you don't care about what I need.

Kevin (rescuer): I do. You know that. I'm really proud of how well you're doing.

Shannon (victim): I have to do everything. That's the problem. Work all day, take care of the house, go to meetings. And then my own boyfriend doesn't support me.

Kevin (persecutor): Come off it! Who fixed the bathroom faucet? Who came running over when you locked yourself out last week? You don't appreciate anything. That's your problem.

Shannon (victim): If you really loved me, you'd be glad to do those things.

Kevin (rescuer): I do love you. I like taking care of things to please you.

Shannon (persecutor): So you say. I think you just like to have things to throw in my face.

Kevin (victim): No matter what I do, it's never enough. Sometimes I just feel like giving up.

Shannon (rescuer): I'm sorry. I know I should show more

appreciation. I've just been on edge lately. I just want you to feel better.

Kevin (persecutor): It would be nice if you'd learn to show it.

Shannon (victim): And it would be nice if you'd learn to be more considerate . . .

The conversation could go on like this for hours, with both people feeling unappreciated and misunderstood. In the meantime, the real issues don't get resolved. Shannon needs Kevin to be more financially responsible and more accepting of her need to go to meetings. Kevin needs Shannon to reassure him that he is important to her. They both need to find ways to nurture their relationship. But none of this can happen when they're caught up in the Drama Triangle.

Interactions like this happen all too often in our daily lives. Instead of trying to find solutions to our problems, we compete to cast ourselves as the injured party—for it is the victim who plays the starring role in the Drama Triangle. When the victim bows out, the drama collapses.

A psychologist I once consulted said that one of the surest routes to emotional health is to let go of the idea that any consenting adult is actually a victim in a relationship. "Sometimes people hurt us or let us down. That doesn't make us a victim. That's part of life," he said. "Being a victim means being helpless, not having a choice. But we all have choices in how we respond to other people, where we focus our attention, what we do with our emotions. Playing the victim keeps relationships stuck and prevents us from moving forward."

When we are the victim, we are not responsible for our choices or our actions. Someone else is to blame, and someone else has the duty to make things better.

In our past, we have undoubtedly been genuinely victimized by people we trusted. When we were children, we were victimized by people who had power over us. As adults with unhealed trauma, we were victimized by people who exploited our confusion and fear. Now, as women who are healing, we are moving beyond the role of victim.

We accept responsibility for our actions, make choices that nurture us, and refuse to accept hurtful or demeaning behavior from others.

Being a victim distracts us from our responsibility to live our life to the best of our ability. When we no longer see ourselves as a victim, we close the curtain on the Drama Triangle and set the stage for emotional growth and healthier relationships.

Handling Our Anger, Finding Forgiveness

No relationship runs smoothly all the time. We humans are much too emotionally complicated for that. But two dynamics in particular can cause confusion in relationships: the experience of anger and the process of forgiveness.

We may have gotten the impression that anger is bad and forgiveness is good. As a result, when someone upsets us we may want to jump over the anger and get to forgiveness right away in the mistaken belief that that's the healthy thing to do. But in fact, both anger and forgiveness have a legitimate role in relationships. It's what we do with them that matters.

Anger: A Valuable Signal

Many of us never learned how to handle our anger. Society has long harbored a double standard that says it's okay for men to be angry, but not women—anger is unfeminine. We're taught that where there is conflict, our role is to be the peacemaker. What's more, many of us are afraid of our anger, fearing that we'll lose control or turn people against us if we let it surface. So we try to suppress feelings of anger. The result? Resentments build up, or we damage our health, or our anger bubbles over in inappropriate ways.

A few years ago, a friend of mine consulted a therapist for help with her marital problems. Her husband had a habit of belittling her with petty criticisms. Usually, she let them roll off her back, but sometimes she retaliated with angry outbursts. When that happened, he accused her of having "anger issues."

She expected the therapist to offer suggestions for controlling her anger. Instead, she was told that her anger was the healthy side of her. Allowing anyone, including her husband, to belittle her was to accept an unhealthy assault on her self-esteem. Instead of trying to ignore or stifle her anger, she needed to resolve the issues that were causing it.

Her therapist's point was that anger signals that something is wrong: Our boundaries are being violated, our trust is being broken, or our self-respect is being battered. Anger is usually a response to hurt. When someone hurts us, it's normal to feel angry.

Problems arise when our anger gets in the way of addressing what is hurting us. When we retaliate with hurtful words of our own, resort to name-calling, or become violent, our anger works against us. Instead of finding ways to deal with its cause, we let our anger itself become an issue. The underlying cause gets ignored, and things escalate from bad to worse.

There are many nonconfrontational ways to vent anger: take a walk, work out at the gym, wash the car, clean the windows—whatever it takes to release the energy that builds up when we're angry. More importantly, though, we need to pay attention to the cause of our anger and use it as an impetus for change.

In my friend's case, she used "I" statements to clearly and calmly tell her husband how hurt she was by his constant put-downs. She made it clear that she wanted him to go to marriage counseling with her so they could both learn better ways to communicate with each other. Together, they worked on addressing some of the underlying issues that were making them both unhappy. She used her anger as a tool to initiate positive change.

Dealing with our anger is no guarantee of better relationships—after all, we're only one half of the relationship equation. But when we are willing to tackle the root causes of our anger directly, we create an atmosphere in which more honest and empathetic relationships are possible.

Forgiveness: Letting Go of Anger

When I was young, I worked briefly with an older woman whose thirteen-year-old daughter had been murdered years earlier. Her gentle eyes full of sadness, the woman told me that she had forgiven the man who killed her child. I remember being taken aback. How could anyone forgive someone for murdering her child? How was that even possible?

I still wonder about it sometimes when I think about the complexities of forgiveness. Why can some of us forgive the most terrible acts, while others harbor lifelong grudges for seemingly trivial offenses? The truth is, forgiveness is highly personal. There are no set rules to guide us. Since we humans are flawed and inevitably make mistakes, there will be many times over the course of our lives when we will extend—and seek—forgiveness. But what does it actually mean to forgive?

To begin with, forgiveness is not saying that a wrong that was done is okay or that it no longer matters. Some wrongs will never be okay. Whether we choose to forgive or not, there is no changing the fact that we were hurt, we were scarred, and we will carry this wound for the rest of our life. Some wrongs are that deep.

But that doesn't mean that severe wrongs can never be forgiven. Because forgiveness is not necessarily about the depth of the wound. Forgiveness simply means that we, the wounded, no longer carry anger or resentment in our heart. We no longer expect a debt to be paid.

Sometimes it is easier to forgive if we believe that the person who harmed us was unaware of the harm being done. Jesus' words on the cross—"Forgive them, Father, for they know not what they do"—point out that wounds are sometimes the result of human ignorance or confusion. The French saying *Tout comprendre c'est tout pardonner*—"To understand all is to forgive all"—suggests that there may be mitigating circumstances in the life of someone who commits a harmful act; that if we understand the whole story, we are more likely to forgive. Often, we are more inclined to forgive if the offending person takes responsibility for the action, sincerely apologizes, and tries to make amends.

In the end, though, forgiveness is less about the person who committed the wrong and more about our self. Forgiveness frees us from the destructive impact of festering anger and smoldering resentments. It takes power away from the offender and puts it back in our hands. In some ways, forgiveness is a bit like detachment: We accept that something wrong happened and it's not going to change, but we're not going to carry it with us anymore. We'll let the anger go and move on.

As a result of forgiveness, our relationships can continue to grow despite the mistakes we all make from time to time. Sometimes, mistakes and forgiveness can even bring people closer together in a deepened, mutual understanding and compassion. On the other hand, some wounds are so deep that they signal the end of the relationship. Even if we choose to forgive, the trust that forms the basis of all healthy relationships is irrevocably broken.

As we consider the meaning and complexities of forgiveness, it's worth noting that the person we often find hardest to forgive is our self. We tend to magnify our mistakes, judge ourselves without mercy, and tell ourselves we're horrible people. In reality, our flaws and frailties are no greater or less than those of others. Our goal is not to be perfect, but to accept responsibility for our actions, apologize when we are wrong, and make amends wherever possible.

In the words of the poet Maya Angelou:

> I don't know if I continue, even today, always liking
> myself. But what I learned to do many years ago was
> to forgive myself. It is very important for every human
> being to forgive herself or himself because if you live,
> you will make mistakes—it is inevitable. But once you
> do and you see the mistake, then you forgive yourself

and say, "Well, if I'd known better I'd have done better," that's all. So you say to people who you think you may have injured, "I'm sorry," and then you say to yourself, "I'm sorry."[37]

Forgiveness of others can create a powerful bond that helps hold our relationships together. Forgiveness of our self is an essential part of the healing process. Ultimately, forgiveness is an act of generosity, of self-preservation, and of grace.

Rebuilding Trust

Relationships are complicated, none more so than our relationships with our family.

Many of us were severely hurt by parents and other family members who should have protected us. Often, we were wounded unintentionally by people who struggled with their own mental health issues or who lacked the maturity to fulfill their responsibilities to us. Some of us were raised by parents who were too stunted in their own growth to give us the love and security we needed. And some of us were the victims of outright neglect and abuse.

As we progress in our healing, we eventually face the questions of if, when, and to what extent we should try to heal relationships with family members. There is no right answer to those questions. Some of it depends on where we are in our recovery—and some of it depends on where they are in theirs.

In our early recovery, we naturally focus on our self. We work to understand our past and replace destructive behaviors with healthy ones. We may not feel ready to reconnect with family members who have hurt us or who may try to cast us in our scapegoat role. We may need to walk our own path for a long time before our healthy sense of self is strong enough to withstand a potentially painful encounter.

Even then, we may decide against reestablishing a certain relationship. If the person who hurt us has not acknowledged responsibility and hasn't tried to make amends, we may choose to sever the family tie. Our primary consideration should be, *What will promote my recovery?*

Sometimes, an encounter with someone who hurt us deeply provides a sense of closure even if we don't want a relationship with that person. Sometimes, unexpectedly, we gain new understanding that eases the pain of our past. Sometimes, if both people are committed to healing it, we are able to build a new relationship based on compassion and forgiveness. And if we do, we will need to build a new trust based on the belief that the person will not hurt us again. This will likely take a great deal of patience, honesty, and time. Trust, once broken, does not return easily. But it can return.

Of course, there is another side to the issue of broken trust. During the years of our addiction, we almost certainly inflicted pain on people who love us. We almost certainly broke their trust.

Now that we are recovering, we may long to regain that trust. But the wounds we caused may be too deep and the disappointments too numerous for trust to come easily to the people we love. Even if we're working a Twelve Step program and made a list of the people we've wronged and made our amends in Steps Eight and Nine, trust doesn't automatically result.

One woman recalled telling her children that she was about to receive her first-year sobriety coin in AA, only to hear, "Congratulations. Let us know when you get your coin next year." They told her the same thing when she got her second-year coin. It wasn't until a year later that her children were finally willing to attend the meeting with her. Her son and daughter presented their mother her three-year coin.

"It took that long for them to believe that I was finally serious about recovery," she said. "It took that long to regain their trust."

Grace, who lost custody of four of her children when she was battling addiction, has reestablished relationships with all but one daughter, who continues to reject her. "She's hurt. I understand,"

Grace says. "It makes me very sad, but all I can do is continue to tell her how sorry I am and let her know that I love her. I'm here for her if she needs me."

After many years of estrangement, Tiny has reestablished her relationship with her two children. There was a time when they would see her on a street corner, and they'd go by as if she were a total stranger, "That hurt," she says. "And just the fact that they're in my life today, it's huge. I never thought it was going to happen. I thought my kids were never going to speak to me again."

Tiny says, "I'm proud of the fact that my mom can sleep at night and know where her daughter is. I'm proud that my kids want to be with me. I love the fact that my kids talk to me again and trust me again. They have their own kids and they trust me with them and they want me to be with them. They want me to be around."

Today, Tiny's relationship with her family is the best it has ever been. Getting there required her to take responsibility for her mistakes, to empathize with what her family had gone through, and to find healthier, more honest ways of communicating with them.

Like all healthy relationships, her relationships spring from a place of self-knowledge, self-acceptance, and self-love. "I can actually look in the mirror today and say, 'You deserve better.' I can even say, 'I love you,'" Tiny says with a laugh. "Oh, I love myself!"

Her evident joy—such a stark contrast with the days when she didn't care if she lived or died—is a testament to the miracle of recovery. In his poem "St. Francis and the Sow," Galway Kinnell says we may need "to reteach a thing its loveliness" to help a flower bloom.

Relearning that we are lovely. Allowing the bud of self within us to heal and blossom. Learning to love our self. That's what the process of healing is all about. When we love our self with compassion for our flaws and mistakes and appreciation for all that is good within us, we begin to create the life and relationships that are worthy of who we really are.

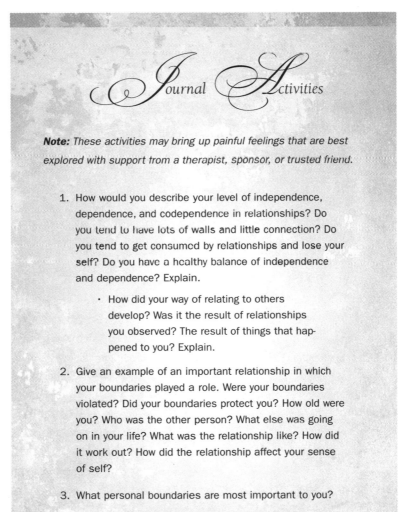

Journal Activities

Note: *These activities may bring up painful feelings that are best explored with support from a therapist, sponsor, or trusted friend.*

1. How would you describe your level of independence, dependence, and codependence in relationships? Do you tend to have lots of walls and little connection? Do you tend to get consumed by relationships and lose your self? Do you have a healthy balance of independence and dependence? Explain.

   - How did your way of relating to others develop? Was it the result of relationships you observed? The result of things that happened to you? Explain.

2. Give an example of an important relationship in which your boundaries played a role. Were your boundaries violated? Did your boundaries protect you? How old were you? Who was the other person? What else was going on in your life? What was the relationship like? How did it work out? How did the relationship affect your sense of self?

3. What personal boundaries are most important to you?

   - List five behaviors that you will not accept from others in a relationship.
   - Now list five behaviors that you require from others in your personal relationships.

4. Describe a damaged family relationship that you would like to give some attention to. Who is this person? What is the nature of the relationship? In what way has it been damaged?

   - What do you hope to get out of addressing this relationship? Do you want to reconnect? Better understand what happened? State your side of the story? Get an apology? Make a final break? Make amends?

   - Write a letter to this family member in which you reveal all your thoughts. Don't mail the letter, but keep it as a guide.

   - When you are ready, reread the letter. Decide what action you want to take, knowing that you can control only your actions, not anybody else's.

5. Our most important relationship is the one we have with our self—for we cannot show others love and compassion unless we feel those in our heart for our self. List ten things you love about yourself. They can be physical, emotional, social, or spiritual traits and qualities.

   - Now list ten more.

7

CARE AND MAINTENANCE OF THE HEALTHY SELF

❦

You are responsible for your life. You can't keep
blaming somebody else for your dysfunction.
Life is really about moving on.

—OPRAH WINFREY,
media personality and philanthropist

Sometimes we have to go back to move forward—not to blame others for our suffering and mistakes, but to see more clearly the fork in the road: we walked down one path for a long time, and now we have chosen another.

The old path—paved with hidden fears and mistaken beliefs—led to pain and self-rejection. The new path—paved with budding courage and growing wisdom—leads to contentment and self-love. It is the path of emotional healing and personal growth.

When we embarked on this journey, we may have hoped to reach a place of perpetual happiness or serenity. But along the way we come to realize that human perfection is not possible, that we all have good days and bad, we all continue to make mistakes, and we all continue to learn.

We discover that the journey itself is our destination.

When we begin to accept that there is no finish line, our attention shifts to where it rightly belongs: to living each day to the best of our ability. For our life does not lie somewhere in our broken past or around the next bend or beyond the horizon. It is here, today, within us, this moment, continually unfolding along the path of our own choosing.

GUIDEPOSTS FOR THE JOURNEY

Our journey is always and forever uniquely our own, but there are tried-and-true guideposts to mark our way. Many women have found the following to be especially helpful:

- Build a support system.
- Develop healthy ways of self-soothing.
- Nurture our talents.
- Find purpose and meaning.
- Deepen our spirituality.

Let's look at each of these in turn.

Build a Support System

"At first it was really hard for me to open up," Tiny said. "I used to be afraid to trust anyone, but little by little I started to let a few people get close to me. Now I love the fact that I have someone I can tell everything to."

No matter how much we may value our independence or how damaged our capacity for trust may be, we all need people we can count on. Having others who care about us is a fundamental human need. We can begin to build a support system in many ways. For example, we can:

- reach out to healthy family members who support our recovery
- find a sponsor in Alcoholics Anonymous or Narcotics Anonymous
- volunteer for housekeeping tasks in our Twelve Step meetings
- volunteer for community organizations that interest us
- join a faith community and actively participate in its programs
- join another kind of support group for a specific issue, such as food or money
- enter a therapeutic relationship with a helpful therapist

As our self-confidence grows, we can take risks and invite people to join us for coffee or a movie or something else we enjoy. Even if we're rejected, we come to realize that although rejection hurts, we can survive it. Then we can take risks again and reach out to others. With time and effort, we will begin to build meaningful friendships and our support system will grow.

Develop Healthy Ways of Self-Soothing

"Yoga has given me a sense of inner peace that I never had before," says Carol. "Any time I feel stressed, I can focus on my breathing or do some of the postures and I immediately feel calmer."

Inner turmoil and difficult emotions are part of life. When we were kids, we may have sucked our thumb or reached for our security blanket when we were stressed. Later, we turned to substances and destructive behaviors for comfort. Now, our task is to replace those negative habits with healthy ones. Watching television is a quick and easy way to distract ourselves, but the violence and negativity of many programs can actually make us feel worse. Instead of automatically turning on the TV when we're under stress, we can develop more positive tools for self-comforting.

In addition to practicing yoga, other popular self-soothing techniques include:

- working out at a gym
- going for a walk or a drive
- taking a warm bath
- sipping herbal tea
- listening to music
- dancing
- writing in our journal
- knitting, crocheting, sewing, or doing other handicrafts
- working in the garden
- cooking a nourishing meal
- reading a good book

- watching an uplifting movie
- talking to a friend
- meditating

What's important to keep in mind is that we have choices about how to respond to stressful situations. We can choose to get caught up in negativity, or we can choose to focus on activities that take our mind off our worries and bring us comfort.

Nurture Our Talents

"My ideal job would involve changing the way society thinks about addiction and the way we treat addicts so that more of us end up in treatment and fewer of us end up in jail," says Grace. "I want to make a difference." She's going to college to prepare for the career she wants.

Like most of us, when Grace was a kid she was often asked, "What do you want to be when you grow up?" She didn't give it much thought during her years of addiction. With sobriety, she realizes that she has the power to envision her future and turn her goals into reality. We all do. It starts with asking ourselves what we enjoy doing and what we're good at, and then finding ways to nurture our abilities. Some of us have natural "people skills" and are good at engaging others. Some of us are good organizers, good speakers, good writers, good artists, good musicians, good caregivers, good healers, good teachers, good cooks, good gardeners, good leaders, and so on.

Whatever our talents, they're an essential part of who we are, a core piece of our authentic self. Our emotional health grows stronger when we nurture our talents to the best of our ability. We can do this in a number of ways: go to college or a vocational training school; take adult education courses at our local school or public library; join a hobby group that promotes shared learning; find related special interest sites on the Internet; network with others who share our interests; buy or rent video programs or books that offer instruction;

set aside quiet time in which to practice our skills. By nurturing our natural gifts, we honor our unique talents, brighten our future, and contribute to the world around us.

Find Purpose and Meaning

"After my marriage ended and I lost custody of my kids, the world felt empty. I had to find something to live for," says Meg. "At first, I focused on my family, on healing those relationships. That's still number one, but I also get a sense of purpose from helping other women get through what I went through. That's important to me."

What am I here for? What am I called to do during my short, precious time on earth? These are among life's biggest questions, questions that must be answered if we are to become the very best version of our authentic self. Finding purpose and meaning requires us to discover what we care deeply about, what touches us at our core, what it is to which we will willingly devote our time, energy, and passion. For many of us, the thing that gives meaning to our life is our children, caring for them, nurturing them, and loving them. For some of us, it's deepening our relationship with our Higher Power. For others, it's contributing to the greater good through volunteering and serving others. Still others find purpose and meaning in creating beauty and harmony in nature, our home or garden, or works of art.

The point is, finding purpose and meaning is a highly individual endeavor—but a critical one. Without a sense of purpose, we often feel lost and adrift, as if nothing matters very much. Our purpose gives us a foundation and a focus, something we can do that matters no matter what. Sometimes we seem to instinctively know what we are called to do. Sometimes we discover our purpose when a life-changing event awakens something inside us. Many of us find our purpose slowly over time as we pay careful attention to our feelings, recognize what moves us deeply, and increasingly devote our time and energy to doing whatever it is that make us feel worthwhile and whole.

Develop Our Spirituality

"When the pain gets strong, I get this fear that I could easily turn into someone who's fat and drunk and spends her days drinking and smoking in front of the TV," Linda confesses. "But my faith has helped me overcome a lot of my fears. It's a source of solace in times of trouble."

Linda has nurtured a deep connection to the god of her understanding. It's a relationship that she turns to again and again for guidance and comfort—an unshakable connection to the everlasting. But spirituality does not require us to believe in a higher being or to practice a particular religion. Instead, spirituality involves a kind of awakening to the fact we are part of something greater than our small self, that the essence of our being is linked to the vast mysterious cosmos and to all living things. With spiritual growth, we become aware that our actions affect not only our self but also everything around us. As a result, we begin to develop a moral code, a code of ethical behavior that helps us take right actions. Spirituality diminishes our sense of separateness and deepens our feelings of compassion, tolerance, and concern for others.

Twelve Step programs are grounded in spiritual principles and promote the spiritual growth of active participants. But there are many other ways to develop our spirituality: we can read the works of spiritual leaders; we can practice meditation and contemplation; we can cultivate a deeper appreciation of nature; we can participate in faith-based communities; we can keep a gratitude journal. Whatever path we choose, our growing spirituality enables us to live in harmony with our personal values, make moral choices, speak our truth, and act in ways that reflect the goodness within us.

MOVING FORWARD

Spirituality writer Sharon Salzberg wrote, "The difference between misery and happiness depends on what we do with our attention."[38]

In this one short sentence, she captures an essential truth: The quality of our life is largely determined by what we choose to nurture and cultivate within us.

One of my favorite parables—a story from the Cherokee people—makes a similar point. It tells the story of a young boy who was treated badly by someone he considered a friend. Hurt and angry, he asks his grandfather for advice. The old man nods understandingly and replies.

"I, too, have felt great anger and hatred for those who have harmed me and seem to feel no regret. But hate wears you down and doesn't hurt your enemy. I have struggled with these feelings many times. It's as if there are two wolves inside me. One wolf is good. He is peaceful, compassionate, and wise. He lives in harmony with others. He fights only when it is right to do so. But the other wolf lives in me, too. He is full of anger, jealousy, and self-pity. The smallest thing infuriates him. He cannot think clearly because his anger is so great. But his anger changes nothing. Sometimes it is hard to live with two wolves inside me, for both of them struggle to dominate my spirit."

The boy gazes anxiously into his grandfather's eyes. "Which wolf wins, grandfather?"

The grandfather smiles and quietly replies, "The one I feed."

The one I feed. The one I give my attention to. The choice is ours.

Life is difficult for everyone; it's a continuing cycle of positive and negative experiences. We cannot change the fact that bad things happen, just as we cannot change our traumatic past. What we can change is what we allow to dominate our spirit. When we are controlled by our pain, our fear, our losses, our mistakes, and our grievances, our life naturally revolves around suffering. We make decisions that reflect and reinforce our negative view of life, and our inner light is dimmed.

When we courageously confront our traumatic past, we are free to put it behind us. We don't pretend it didn't happen. We don't put on our rose-colored glasses and pretend that everything is perfect. We simply choose to take from the past those things that make us stronger and wiser—and then we let go of the rest. We choose to focus on our courage, our resilience, our talents, our compassion, our potential, and our blessings—on everything that is good and beautiful within and around us. Then, the unique and lovely self that we were born to be is free to bud, and grow, and blossom.

And our wounded heart can heal.

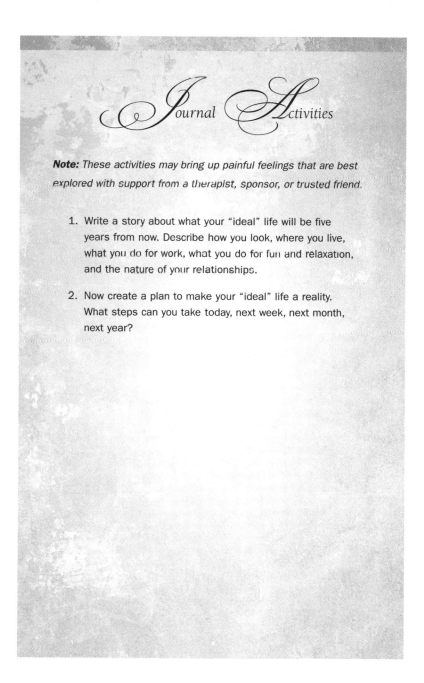

Journal Activities

Note: *These activities may bring up painful feelings that are best explored with support from a therapist, sponsor, or trusted friend.*

1. Write a story about what your "ideal" life will be five years from now. Describe how you look, where you live, what you do for work, what you do for fun and relaxation, and the nature of your relationships.

2. Now create a plan to make your "ideal" life a reality. What steps can you take today, next week, next month, next year?

Appendix: The Twelve Steps of Alcoholics Anonymous

1. We admitted we were powerless over alcohol—that our lives had become unmanageable.

2. Came to believe that a Power greater than ourselves could restore us to sanity.

3. Made a decision to turn our will and our lives over to the care of God *as we understood Him.*

4. Made a searching and fearless moral inventory of ourselves.

5. Admitted to God, to ourselves, and to another human being the exact nature of our wrongs.

6. Were entirely ready to have God remove all these defects of character.

7. Humbly asked Him to remove our shortcomings.

8. Made a list of all persons we had harmed, and became willing to make amends to them all.

9. Made direct amends to such people wherever possible, except when to do so would injure them or others.

10. Continued to take personal inventory and when we were wrong promptly admitted it.

11. Sought through prayer and meditation to improve our conscious contact with God *as we understood Him,* praying only for knowledge of His will for us and the power to carry that out.

12. Having had a spiritual awakening as the result of these steps, we tried to carry this message to alcoholics, and to practice these principles in all our affairs.

Reprinted from *Alcoholics Anonymous*, 4th ed., (New York: Alcoholics Anonymous World Services, 2001), 59–60.

Resources

Recommended Reading

Bancroft, Lundy. *Why Does He Do That?: Inside the Minds of Angry and Controlling Men.* New York: Penguin Group, 2002.

Brown, Brene. *The Gifts of Imperfection: Let Go of Who You Think You're Supposed to Be and Embrace Who You Are.* Center City, MN: Hazelden, 2010.

Brown, Stephanie. *A Place Called Self: Women, Sobriety, and Radical Transformation.* Center City, MN: Hazelden, 2004.

Brown, Stephanie. *A Place Called Self: Companion Workbook.* Center City, MN: Hazelden, 2006.

Casey, Karen. *Each Day a New Beginning: Daily Meditations for Women.* Center City, MN: Hazelden, 1982.

Covington, Stephanie. *A Healing Journey: A Workbook for Women (Healing Trauma Workbook).* Center City, MN: Hazelden, 1994.

Covington, Stephanie. *A Woman's Way through the Twelve Steps.* Center City, MN: Hazelden, 1994.

Covington, Stephanie. *A Woman's Way through the Twelve Steps Workbook.* Center City, MN: Hazelden, 2010.

Dayton, Tian. *Trauma and Addiction: Ending the Cycle of Pain through Emotional Literacy.* Deerfield Beach, FL: Health Communications, Inc., 2000.

Hunter, Joanna V. *But He'll Change: End the Thinking That Keeps You in an Abusive Relationship.* Center City, MN: Hazelden, 2010.

Iliff, Brenda. *A Woman's Guide to Recovery.* Center City, MN: Hazelden, 2008.

Knapp, Caroline. *Drinking: A Love Story.* New York: Dial Press, 2005.

Norwood, Robin. *Women Who Love Too Much: When You Keep Wishing and Hoping He'll Change.* New York: Pocket Books, 2008.

Salzberg, Sharon. *Lovingkindness: The Revolutionary Art of Happiness.* Boston: Shambhala, 1997.

Other Helpful Resources

Helpguide
www.helpguide.org
This nonprofit organization offers expert, ad-free resources to help people resolve health challenges.

National Coalition Against Domestic Violence
www.ncadv.org
The NCADV's mission is to organize for collective power by advancing transformative work, thinking, and leadership of communities and individuals working to end the violence in our lives.

Resource Center to Promote Acceptance, Dignity, and Social Inclusion Associated with Mental Health
www.promoteacceptance.samhsa.gov
800-540-0320
A service of the U.S. government's Substance Abuse and Mental Health Services Administration (SAMHSA), this resource center counters prejudice and discrimination associated with mental illness by
- gathering information and research
- providing technical assistance and support

Women's Prison Association Institute on Women and Criminal Justice
www.wpaonline.org/institute
This national policy center is dedicated to
- reforming **policy and practice** affecting women in the criminal justice system
- publishing timely **research and information** on criminal justice-involved women
- serving as a **resource for policymakers, media, and the public** concerned about women and justice
- supporting the **voices of women who've experienced incarceration** in advocating for change

NOTES

1 Elizabeth Weise, "The Secret Lives of Female Alcoholics," *USA Today,* September 15, 2009, http://usatoday.com/news/health/2009 -09-14-women-alcoholism_N.htm.

2 Caroline Knapp, *Drinking: A Love Story* (New York: Dial Press, 2005), 193.

3 "Mother Blues—Child Blues: How Maternal Depression Affects Children," *NYU Child Study Center Letter* 7, no. 3 (January/February 2003).

4 Vivien Prior and Danya Glaser, *Understanding Attachment and Attachment Disorders: Theory, Evidence and Practice* (Philadelphia: Jessica Kingsley Publishers, 2006), 30–31.

5 Simone de Beauvoir, *The Second Sex,* trans. and ed. H. M. Parshley (New York: Bantam Books, 8th printing, 1965), 314.

6 Sarah Showfety, "Field Guide to the Tomboy: High Heels and Pink? No Way," *Psychology Today,* September 1, 2008, www. psychologytoday.com/articles/200809/field-guide-the-tomboy-high-heels-and-pink-no-way.

7 Advocates for Youth, "Child Sexual Abuse I: An Overview," 2008, www.advocatesforyouth.org/publications/410?task=view.

8 de Beauvoir, *The Second Sex,* 308.

9 Tian Dayton, *Trauma and Addiction: Ending the Cycle of Pain Through Emotional Literacy* (Deerfield Beach, FL: Health Communications, 2000), 4.

10 Angie Panos, "Healing from the Shame Associated with Traumatic Events." *Gift from Within: PTSD Resources for Survivors and Care-givers,* June 2002, www.giftfromwithin.org/html/healing.html.

11 Panos, "Healing from the Shame."

12 Caron Zlotnick, Jennifer Johnson, et al., "Childhood trauma, trauma in adulthood, and psychiatric diagnosis." National Institutes of Health, NIH Public Access Author Manuscript, October 2007, www.ncbi.nlm.nih.gov/pmc/articles/PMC2648973.

13 Christine Heim, Bekh Bradley, et al., "Effect of Childhood Trauma on Adult Depression and Neuroendocrine Function: Sex-Specific Moderation by CRH Receptor 1 Gene," *Frontiers in Behavioral Neuroscience,* November 2009, www.frontiersin.org/behavioral _neuroscience/10.3389/neuro.08.041.2009/full.

14 Joseph Volpicelli, Geetha Balaraman, et al. "The Role of Uncontrollable Trauma in the Development of PTSD and Alcohol Addiction," *Alcohol Research and Health* 23, no. 4 (1999), 260. National Institute on Alcohol Abuse and Alcoholism, http://pubs.niaaa.nih.gov /publications/arh23-4/256-262.pdf.

15 "Topics in Brief: Drugs, Brains, and Behavior—The Science of Addiction," National Institute on Drug Abuse, 2007, www. drugabuse.gov/publications/topics-in-brief/drugs-brains-behavior -science-addiction.

16 "Childhood Trauma and Depression," *Observer* 23, no. 6 (July/ August 2010), Association for Psychological Science, www. psychologicalscience.org/index.php/publications/observer/2010 /july-august-10/childhood-trauma-and-depression.html.

17 Kate Johnson, "Childhood Sexual Abuse Alters Female Brain Structure," Medscape Medical News, April 19, 2012, www. medscape.com/viewarticle/762354.

18 Dayton, *Trauma and Addiction,* 102.

19 Knapp, Drinking: *A Love Story,* 75.

20 "Handbook for Prison Managers and Policymakers on Women and Imprisonment," Criminal Justice Handbook Series (New York: United Nations Office on Drugs and Crime, 2008), 19, www. unodc.org/documents/justice-and-prison-reform/women-and -imprisonment.pdf.

21 Ibid.

22 Robin Norwood, *Women Who Love Too Much,* (New York: Pocket Books, 2008), 90.

23 Stephanie Brown, *A Place Called Self* Hazelden (Center City, MN, 2004), 139.

24 Knapp, *Drinking: A Love Story,* 60.

25 Norwood, 23.

26 Lundy Bancroft, *Why Does He Do That? Inside the Minds of Angry and Controlling Men* (New York: Penguin Group, 2002), 107.

27 Domestic Violence Statistics, 2012, http://domesticviolencestatistics .org/domestic-violence-statistics/.

28 Bancroft, *Why Does He Do That?*, 177.

29 Knapp, *Drinking: A Love Story*, 77.

30 Melissa Hunt, interview with Medscape Medical News (Kate Johnson, "Childhood Sexual Abuse Alters Female Brain Structure," April 19, 2012, www.medscape.com/viewarticle/762354). Dr. Hunt is associate director of clinical training in the psychology department at the University of Pennsylvania in Philadelphia.

31 Brown, *A Place Called Self*, 8.

32 Claude Steiner, *Achieving Emotional Literacy* (London: Bloomsbury, 1997), 11.

33 "Eight Dimensions of Wellness: A Holistic Guide to Physical and Mental Wellness," Substance Abuse and Mental Health Services Administration, September 2011, www.promoteacceptance.samhsa .gov/10by10/dimensions.aspx.

34 Zorka Hereford, "Healthy Personal Boundaries and How to Establish Them," Essential Life Skills.net, www.esssentiallifeskills.net /personalboundaries.html.

35 Sharon Salzberg, *Lovingkindness: The Revolutionary Art of Happiness* (Boston: Shambhala, 1997), 170.

36 Karpman first described the Drama Triangle in his 1968 article "Fairy Tales and Script Drama Analysis," *Transactional Analysis Bulletin* 7 (26), 39-43.

37 Quoted on "Good Reads" website, www.goodreads.com/quotes /169703-i-don-t-know-if-i-continue-even-today-always-liking.

38 Sharon Salzberg, *Lovingkindness*, 12.

ABOUT THE AUTHOR

BEVERLY CONYERS began writing about addiction in response to her daughter's struggles with substance abuse. The author of *Addict in the Family: Stories of Loss, Hope, and Recovery* and *Everything Changes: Help for Families of Newly Recovering Addicts*, she lives in Massachusetts, where she teaches in a community college. She continues to learn about addiction and recovery and increasingly focuses on spiritual growth.

About Hazelden Publishing

As part of the Hazelden Betty Ford Foundation, Hazelden Publishing offers both cutting-edge educational resources and inspirational books. Our print and digital works help guide individuals in treatment and recovery, as well as their loved ones.

Professionals who work to prevent and treat addiction also turn to Hazelden Publishing for evidence-based curricula, digital content solutions, and videos for use in schools, treatment and correctional programs, and community settings. We also offer training for implementation of our curricula.

Through published and digital works, Hazelden Publishing extends the reach of healing and hope to individuals, families, and communities affected by addiction and related issues.

For information about Hazelden publications
please call **800-328-9000**
or visit us online at **hazelden.org/bookstore**.